Late-Stage Babylon

Late-Stage Babylon

Angie Speaks

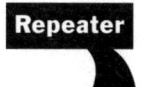

Published by Repeater Books

An imprint of Watkins Media Ltd

Unit 11 Shepperton House

89-93 Shepperton Road

London

N1 3DF

United Kingdom

www.repeaterbooks.com

A Repeater Books paperback original 2025

1

Distributed in the United States by Random House, Inc., New York.

ISBN: 9781917516006

Ebook ISBN: 9781917516013

The manufacturer's authorised representative in the EU for product safety is: eucomply OÜ - Pärnu mnt 139b-14, 11317 Tallinn, Estonia, hello@eucompliancepartner.com, www.eucompliancepartner.com

Printed and bound by CPI Group (UK) Ltd, Croydon, CR0 4YY

"The light shines in the darkness, and the darkness does not comprehend it — yet the light does not flee." - John 1:5

Contents

Introduction:
The Ontological Shock

"The dead came back from Jerusalem, where they found not what they sought."

These are the opening lines of *Seven Sermons to the Dead*, a visionary work by C.G. Jung — psychologist, mystic, and reluctant prophet. Spoken through his inner guide Philemon — an Angel with Kingfisher wings — the *Sermons* offer a hidden gospel to a post-sacred age, channeled during a time of deep personal crisis and transformation. The *"dead,"* as Jung came to understand, are not the departed but the living — contemporary people cut off from meaning, myth, and the holy.

Few texts in modern psychology bridge the archaic and the contemporary so powerfully, offering not just sacred insight but a compass for those adrift in the cold machinery of a disenchanted world. The dead returned from the holy city still empty, still searching. Philemon answered, and through him Jung gave voice to truths buried beneath the surface of modern life. Part analyst, part oracle, C.G. Jung channeled the *Seven Sermons* during a transcendent encounter in 1916. One night, his famous home in Switzerland was filled with an eerie atmosphere, as if crowded with spirits. He, his family, and even his servants felt the presence of something otherworldly. As the tension reached its peak, Jung reported hearing a distinct knock on his front door, despite there being no one outside.

In response to this strange encounter, Jung retreated into his study, where the *Seven Sermons to the Dead* poured out of him like living water, a multilayered cosmology paired with philosophical and spiritual reckoning with the crisis of modern times. Like the biblical Jacob, Jung — a man of science, reason, and modernity, and a world-renowned psychologist — wrestled with God.

As Jung was nearing the end of his life, he felt his soul torn between two great opposites — a struggle he saw mirrored in the fractured psyches and war-torn, twentieth-century world around him. These opposites were knowledge and faith. As a man of science, the founder of analytical psychology, and a foundational figure in the study of the unconscious, knowledge had shaped his domain, his persona, his reputation. But the deeper he ventured into the mystery of the psyche, the more he was drawn toward the ineffable, the unexplainable, the numinous, and the holy. His inner division reflected a deeper cultural rift — a world of the twentieth century, fraught with war, mechanization, and political strife, caught between reason and revelation, progress and meaning, mechanism and myth. Faith began to pull at his soul like an anvil, dragging him into uncharted depths. The *Seven Sermons* became his crucible, where the impossible polarities that defined both his life and his era collided.

During the lockdown summer of 2021, I was visited by the same spirits that visited Jung. Like many in the world, I was undergoing my own sacred crisis. I was nearing the end of my twenties, trailing the wreckage of a career in commentary and journalism. The world felt dead — and so did I. Like the dead in the *Seven Sermons*, I had come back from Jerusalem and found not what I had sought there.

The deluge came for me, and I had nothing left to hide behind. Friends lost, disillusioned with political spaces I once belonged to, I was drifting in the ontological desert — among "the dead."

Just a few years earlier, I had been a rising voice on the You-Tube left — a strange digital ecosystem of pop culture critics, video essayists, and livestreamers who fused politics with performance. It was the millennial echo of the 1960s — idealistic, chaotic, and brittle. The Bernie era, which for a time gave us the illusion of purpose and collective momentum, eventually collapsed. In its place came infighting, betrayal, and a kind of soft ideological authoritarianism that had little patience for complexity or inner work.

Advocacy for socialism became hollow — absorbed by identity management, institutional ambition, and the language of moral purity. The shock of that disillusionment wasn't just political — it was a paradigm shift. The movements of my twenties evaporated, and the contradictions that had always been present finally erupted into view.

Like Jung, I found myself caught between opposing forces. But where his struggle was between faith and knowledge, mine emerged as a tension between belonging and sovereignty. I could feel the pull toward ideological possession, the safety of the collective narrative, but something in me resisted. I wanted to understand — not just how the left had failed politically, but what deeper forces had brought it to such impotence and spiritual exhaustion. Very few wanted to hold that tension or even name it. We, like so many before us, had come back from Jerusalem and found not what we sought — and now stood silently among the dead.

In the *Seven Sermons*, Philemon — Jung's inner guide and the embodiment of his Logos — is confronted by a horde of the dead. These are not just any dead, but the restless souls of those shaped by the modern world: products of the twentieth and twenty-first centuries, born into an era of rapid techno-logical upheaval and spiritual dislocation. Unlike earlier souls, they are caught in a unique bind — the unresolved tension between faith and knowledge. In previous eras, this conflict was buried deep in the collective unconscious; now it stands at the center of our modern crisis.

According to the mythic logic of the *Sermons*, when such existential dilemmas remain unresolved, they bind the soul, preventing it from moving on. And in an age where the rec-onciliation of opposing forces in our psyches and in the wider culture is rarely undertaken — let alone honored — modern souls become trapped in a kind of psychic limbo. What Ti-betan Buddhists call the *Bardo* in the *Book of the Dead*, Jung intuited as the state of the wandering dead: adrift, unmoored, suspended between worlds.

Philemon, angel of mercy, meets them in this liminal space — not with condemnation, but with teaching. He helps them hold the paradox, face their fragmentation, and pass through. In this way, the *Seven Sermons* becomes a metaphor for all of us who find ourselves in the in-between: in collapse, in crisis, in the threshold places where old meaning has died but the new has not yet emerged. When we enter the desert of the dead — when the world as we knew it dissolves — there are still voices that call to us. Angels of mercy whisper at the edge of liminality, if only we are open enough to listen.

At a time in my life when I was overcome with the need to self-reflect, many of my peers in political spaces grew more radicalized — swept away by the culture war's siren call and swallowed by the zero-sum dialectic of left versus right. What might appear from the outside as fringe — the edgy commentators, niche YouTubers, disillusioned essayists, and irony-drenched "take havers" of the internet — has become, in truth, the frontline of ideological production. These fringes are not marginal anymore. They are the new psychic engines of our political and spiritual weather systems. Memes, moods, and Vibe Shifts aren't trivial — they're modern vectors of ontology. They shape elections, collapse old myths, and usher in new psychic configurations before most people even know what hit them.

"The Vibe Shift," often treated as a winking euphemism for post-Trump cultural reordering, is in reality a misdiagnosis of something deeper. It signals an intense rupture in how we relate to truth, meaning, identity, and one another in this time. Over the last decade, many of us have been forced to confront our own hypocrisies, contradictions, and projections. For the left in particular, this meant facing the authoritarian shadows it long believed belonged only to its enemies. Freedom of speech, bodily autonomy, and countercultural rebellion — once hallmarks of leftist identity — became, during the pandemic and beyond, positions increasingly associated with the right. Meanwhile, the left's historic alignment with the working class has eroded as its language became more technocratic, elite, and abstract — focusing on identity performance over material realities. Cultural power has been spent not on solidarity but on posture, purity rituals, and algorithmic self-optimization. The spiritual vocabulary of faith, family, safety, and symbolic meaning — once sneered at as regressive — found renewed resonance on the right, leaving the left disenchanted, laundered through corporate neoliberalism, and often unable to inspire the very people it claims to represent.

This shift has been disorienting for many and has opened a fork in the road: double down on ideological possession — clinging to a collapsing worldview with no mythic ground — or open ourselves, painfully, to reflection, reconciliation, and restoration. In the thick of this reckoning, I also found myself disoriented and raw. And like many others walking through the ruins of certainty, I reached for voices that had already passed through the fire. Not because they offered easy answers, but because they had the courage to name the virus without mistaking its costume.

For me, when the walls finally caved in — when the party lines blurred and the moral noise got too loud to think — I stopped trying to belong and started listening again. Toni Morrison was one of those voices. A rare one. She saw past the branding, past the noise. She *knew*. In her 1995 essay "Racism and Fascism," she warned us:

> Conservative, moderate, liberal; right, left, hard left, far right; religious, secular, socialist — we must not be blindsided by these Pepsi-Cola, Coca-Cola labels because the genius of fascism is that any political structure can host the virus.

It wasn't fascism in the historical sense she was pointing to — it was the deeper pattern: authoritarianism. That creeping, soul-flattening virus that can wear any mask, wave any flag, speak any language. That psychic parasite that uses morality as a cudgel and certainty as a shield. It doesn't care if you're left or right. It only cares that you stop thinking and stop asking questions.

Like Wetiko: the Native American concept of a parasitic mind-virus that deceives its host by pretending to help while secretly feeding on the soul — authoritarianism survives by shapeshifting, adapting its appearance to exploit trust and evade detection. During the Trump era, the Biden years, and the surreal clampdown of the COVID regime, I watched this virus jump hosts. I saw Big Tech fuse with liberal moralism, watched dissenters erased in the name of safety, and witnessed a cynical elite co-opt collective trauma for clout. I saw identity weaponized, speech stifled, and friends I once marched beside turn into judges and enforcers for the machine.

I refused to play along. I wouldn't betray the part of me that still saw the *truth*, even if it wasn't algorithmically sound. And I paid the price.

Morrison saw all this coming. She saw it long before I was even born. And the ache in her voice when she wrote about the spiritual and material starvation in times like these, when the authoritarian shadow flares up on all sides — it broke me. She named the persecution. The absorption. The pressure to conform. The loss of silence, mystery, and care. Everything I was going through and witnessing, she'd already mapped.

We are witnessing a shift, not just in politics but in the collective psyche itself. We are living through a spiritual crisis, and while many are dragged deeper into the desert of the dead, chasing new ideologies, new trends, old skins, there are still those who wait at the crossroads.

These are strange times, and the tides of ideological upheaval and shifting paradigms have not spared our public figures, intellectuals, or celebrities. Russell Brand, once the poster boy for sex, drugs, and anti-establishment irreverence, now speaks the language of Orthodox Christianity. Richard Dawkins, the arch-atheist who once declared religion a virus of the mind, recently defended "cultural Christianity" as a civilizational stabilizer for a period of Western collapse. Ayaan Hirsi Ali — long a champion of Enlightenment secularism and a critic of religious dogma — has very publicly converted to Christianity. Even alt-model and goth makeup mogul Kat Von D, once synonymous with occult aesthetics, has renounced witchcraft and embraced baptism. Whether these shifts are rooted in faith, politics, or brand recalibration can be debated — but what's undeniable is that they mirror a broader societal swing away from secular certainties and toward much older, symbolic containers.

We're witnessing a hunger for meaning that the smug rationalism of the old liberal consensus simply can't satisfy. The old "Jerusalem" has fallen. The COVID pandemic didn't just disrupt daily life — it exposed a profound crisis of legitimacy. Institutions that once appeared stable and trustworthy — governments, media outlets, universities, scientific bodies — revealed themselves to be deeply politicized, fallible, and, at times, outright contemptuous of dissent. "Trust the science" became a mantra not of open inquiry, but of compliance — invoked selectively, weaponized to silence inconvenient questions, and retroactively edited when narratives shifted. Official guidelines changed overnight with little explanation. Once-taboo theories were quietly rehabilitated. Those who voiced doubt or nuance were decried as conspiracists or grifters. The result wasn't just confusion — it was epistemic betrayal.

For many, this rupture triggered something deeper than political disillusionment. It undermined the foundational belief that the world is knowable, manageable, and progressing toward something better through the application of reason and expertise: Jung's crisis of faith and knowledge rearing its head once more in the twenty-first century. The liberal secular worldview — confident in its own neutrality, propped up by technocratic gatekeepers, allergic to metaphysical ambiguity — suddenly looked brittle, inadequate, even dishonest. And in its place, people began to search for other maps: faith-based, religious, traditional, nationalist, conspiracy frameworks, ancestral lineages, or symbolic cosmologies that offered a sense of coherence and purpose in a world that now felt chaotic and duplicitous.

For many on the left, especially younger millennials and Gen Z, the breakdown of liberal institutions wasn't metabolized through self-reflection or positive change but was met with moral panic, censorship, and a doubling-down on authoritarian elitism. Ironically, the very tools used to suppress "dangerous misinformation" — surveillance, deplatforming, moral purity tests — mirrored the authoritarian tendencies they claimed to oppose. Meanwhile, the populist right, emboldened by this overreach, mirrored that authoritarianism in their own key: restricting civil liberties, targeting dissent, and stoking a vengeful politics of *ressentiment*. And here we are again, in the thick of a new Trump regime, one that's not merely ideologically dangerous but increasingly authoritarian in its methods: banning books, threatening journalists, and restricting reproductive freedoms. The two sides reflect each other like inverted masks, each accusing the other of tyranny while becoming what they claim to despise. This is not just political decay; it's spiritual decay.

For many, especially those raised under the comforting umbrella of secular liberalism, the post-2016 vibe shift was their first taste of epistemological collapse. But for those of us raised in faith traditions — as I was — the unraveling of a worldview is an old wound. The period around COVID, the previous collapse of the Bernie Sanders campaign, and the disillusionment with the left pulled me into a familiar darkness. It reminded me of being seventeen and watching the God of my childhood dissolve — the hollow space it left behind, the terror of unknowing, the temptation to grab hold of anything that promised coherence.

What I saw in myself then, I now see everywhere. Many who never knew the loss of a myth — the death of a God, the betrayal of a guiding narrative — were and are now experiencing this for the first time. But instead of sitting with the tension, as real transformation demands, many lunged toward the nearest ideology, tradition, or algorithmically optimized identity that might soothe the ache. Some turned to religion. Some to nationalism. Some to activism as a surrogate spirituality. Others, tragically, simply hardened into nihilistic cynicism.

But I recognized the look — the flicker of hunger behind the forced conviction. I knew what it meant to be grasping for meaning not from faith, but from desperation. And because I had already passed through that fire, I could pause. I didn't need to lunge. I could be a witness instead.

The smug confidence of Enlightenment rationalism and secular progressivism has given way to something cold, brittle, and punitive. What emerged during the pandemic wasn't simply authoritarian overreach or political hysteria — it was, in Jung's terms, a manifestation of the *antimimon pneuma*, the counterfeit spirit. The first Trump era, followed by the madness of the COVID years, shattered illusions of stability, reason, and humanism — core tenets of the secular liberal project.

People all over the spectrum didn't just change their minds — they became radical converts. I watched people abandon former selves with religious fury. Even the late-night jesters of the liberal court became inquisitors: Jimmy Kimmel, a "harmless" clown, famously sneered at the sick and unvaccinated, suggesting they be denied health care. "Trust the science" became a kind of techno-orthodox chant, emptied of nuance and enforced with zealotry. You could feel it in the air: a hum of paranoia, moral absolutism, and collective dissociation. It was spiritual inversion. A hatred of life disguised as safety. Human connection demonized. Children muzzled. Everyone isolated, celebrations forbidden. Joy itself became suspect. And beneath it all, the machine kept purring: cold, bureaucratic, efficient. A new orthodoxy was rising — technocratic and lifeless, no less dogmatic than the one it claimed to replace.

This wasn't the secular liberalism I had grown up with. I thought leaving behind the wrath of God meant entering a world of clarity, compassion, and balance. Instead, I was witnessing the jaws of another absolutism — one even more insidious because it wore a mask of progress. It was then that I began to understand what Jung had seen coming.

In *Aion*, Jung's visionary work on the phenomenology of the "Self," he outlines the spiritual consequences of the Christian era's one-sidedness — its refusal to integrate the shadow, its idealization of pure light at the expense of wholeness. That repression, he warned, would not dissipate. It would return in the form of its opposite. This is the psychological law of *enantiodromia* — the turning of things into their opposites. And just as Christianity emerged to temper the brutality of the pagan world, so too did secular liberalism rise in response to the excesses of Christian dogma. But now, our new secular order has started to mirror the same shadows it once remedied and condemned.

Jung called this emerging force the Antichrist — not a literal devil, but a psychic event. As Jung himself said,

The coming of the Antichrist is not just a prophetic prediction — it is an inexorable psychological law whose effect is apparent at the end of an era. The accumulation of all the evil the human soul has held back and repressed during the Christian aeon must eventually pour out and manifest. The Antichrist represents the shadow, the inferior function, the thing that the collective consciousness has rejected.

The *antimimon pneuma*, the "counterfeit spirit," is a distorted double of the sacred. It arises when symbols lose their vitality, when meaning dries up and is replaced by dogma, hysteria, and false idols. In one of his most haunting passages, Jung writes:

If metaphysical ideas no longer have such a fascinating effect as before, this is certainly not due to any lack of primitivity in the European psyche, but simply and solely to the fact that the erstwhile symbols no longer express what is now welling up from the unconscious... This end-result is a true antimimon pneuma, a false spirit of arrogance, hysteria, wooly-mindedness, criminal amorality, and doctrinaire fanaticism... fit only to be fed wholesale to the mass man of today. That is what the post-Christian spirit looks like.

We see it in the cold, technocratic logic that celebrates atomization and disembodiment; in the dehumanizing discourse that turned public health into a tool for social punishment; in the ideological possession that haunts all directions of the political spectrum; in the looming threat of authoritarianism;

in the way meaning itself has been evacuated from the cultural sphere — replaced by performance, algorithm, and outrage. Jung described it perfectly: "*a false spirit of arrogance, hysteria, wooly-mindedness, criminal amorality, and doctrinaire fanaticism… fit only to be fed wholesale to the mass man of today.*"

This is not merely the failure of politics. It is a failure of myth. A crisis of symbol. And it has ushered us into what Jung, in *Seven Sermons to the Dead*, called the domain of the dead — a liminal space where the spirits of the unintegrated past return to haunt the present. The "dead" are not just ancestors or ghosts; they are the unlived lives, the unprocessed traumas, the rejected archetypes, the gods we stopped naming. And now, they're knocking at the door of the collective psyche — demanding to be fed.

During my darkest stretches of the pandemic, I found myself returning to Jung's *Sermons* — not for comfort, but for recognition. I had grown up in a religious world. I knew what it meant to lose an ontological scaffolding. I knew the disorientation, the hunger, the temptation to grasp for anything that could restore meaning. And so when I saw public figures and friends fall into ideological possession — whether through blind compliance, or sudden conversions, or internet-brained cosplay — I didn't judge. I understood. Because I had seen this void before, but I had learned to sit with it.

That's our world now. *Late-Stage Babylon*. A culture gorged on spectacle, yet still starving for meaning.

Jung knew what most of us are only just beginning to realize: that when meaning collapses, the unconscious doesn't disappear — it surges. It floods. It invades the empty spaces left behind by failed myths. And unless we learn to relate to it — to honor it, dialogue with it, integrate it — we risk being devoured by it.

The Antichrist is not coming, It's already here.

For Jung, the Antichrist is not merely an external figure — it is the shadow of an era and the embodiment of profound one-sidedness. It emerges when an aspect of the "Self" is severed, disowned, and left to fester in the unconscious, where it gains autonomy and begins to operate as a complex — disrupting thought, distorting perception, unraveling the soul's orientation toward truth. It is not evil in the cartoonish sense — it is imbalance manifest. A psyche at war with itself.

And yet, within every shadow is a spark. The antidote to one-sidedness — not inversion, but integration. Not a return to dogma, but to wholeness. In the language of symbols, what heals is not the sword, but the spiral — the harmonizing of opposites, the sacred tension of synthesis. Jung understood this as the work of the mediating third, the mysterious force that reconciles the split. He called it by many names. One of them was the Holy Spirit.

Chapter 1

Movement of the Spirit

I was born into a space that throbbed with voltage — something like God, something like illusion. A church hall vibrating with bodies, tongues, and music. My mother was the center of it all — a preacher and a paradox. Former Miss Nigeria turned prophetic firebrand. Beauty queen to spirit-mount. Her transformation was our mythology.

There's something elemental and almost operatic in the arc of her story. A national darling, then a scandal — a public fall, a lynch mob. And then, resurrection: the church. Pentecostalism gave her back her voice, and she wielded it like a sword. But it didn't always erase the pain.

Even as a child, I sensed something was off. The church felt like a performance haunted by something hidden. It was visceral, yes — sweaty, embodied, filled with tongues and convulsions. The Spirit "moved" people, but beneath the power, there was a shadow. The liminal spaces of the church — hallways behind the altar, green rooms where pastors prepped — carried the same eerie charge as the "Backrooms" we now joke about online. Places outside of time, vibrating with the uncanny. Not evil, exactly. Just wrong. Like something posing as holy.

This wasn't the clean world of televangelists with big hair and bigger smiles. This was lower-tier Pentecostalism — frayed carpets, screaming children, cheap suits, plastic flags of Israel. We worshipped with urgency, because the world was ending. The Rapture was imminent, and we had a role to play. I grew up believing history was a countdown that we, the faithful, were midwifing the apocalypse. This made us dangerous in our own quiet way. We didn't just anticipate the end — we longed for it, prayed it forward.

They called it spiritual warfare, but it often looked more like political theater. Zionism was braided into the sermons. Pastor John Hagee, Evangelical firebrand, televangelist, and author of the Bush era's *God's Candidate for America*, became a kind of messianic mascot. I remember waving Israeli flags at his conferences as a child, not really understanding why. It was all so loud, so confusing. The gospel was supposed to be about peace and love, but somehow we were cheering for war in the Middle East. Dominionism hid in plain sight, cloaked in prophecy and patriotism. The pulpit became a delivery system for ideological control.

And yet, the Holy Spirit moved. Somehow. Through all the noise. That's the unbearable tension of it all. Beneath the spectacle, beneath the spiritual abuse and political manipulation, something real flickered. A presence. It's what kept me from fully hating the church, even after I left. It's what makes it hard to write about it now without lapsing into either nostalgia or condemnation.

There was always a duality. The Spirit was there — but so was the counterfeit. I didn't have the words for it then, but I felt it. Something that mimicked divinity while pulling us into a tight, suffocating space. The spirit of control masquerading as freedom. That's the counterfeit pneuma. The anti-spirit. The one that draws you in with the promise of liberation, only to chain you to ideology, dogma, and soul denial. It wears many masks — political, religious, cultural. But it always leaves you smaller than you were before.

As I grew older and stepped into other ideological spaces, I realized the same pattern replicated itself. The left was not immune. In fact, it had its own version of ascensionism — the utopia just beyond the revolution. A promised day when capitalism would fall and the oppressed would rise. It was, in its own way, a secular Rapture. And just like in church, the beautiful ideas — equality, solidarity — were often hijacked by darker impulses. Technocratic accelerationism. Cathartic violence. Ideological purity tests. I watched beautiful visions get calcified into dogma. I watched people justify cruelty in the name of compassion.

I saw how both the evangelical right and the revolutionary left had the potential to house the same archetype: the belief that the end justifies the means, that spiritual or moral authority gives one the right to dominate. It's the malefic Saturnian energy that Carl Jung explored in *Aion* — not just a mythic symbol, but a psychological truth. In alchemy, the planet Saturn, in its shadow form, rules over time, discipline, hierarchy, and control. It governs structure — but when it turns toxic, it becomes prison. It calcifies what should remain in flux. It binds. It punishes. It says: "order is more important than life." The malefic Saturn isn't just some ancient god — it's the part of the psyche that fears chaos so much that it kills spirit to preserve system. It lives in bureaucracies, in religious legalism, in authoritarian ideologies, in the icy hands of technocrats. When Saturn rules unbalanced, soul suffocates.

That's what terrified me most: realizing that the Antichrist was never an external figure. He's the algorithm. He's the pulpit. He's the technocrat, the influencer, the Silicon Valley utopian. He's the part of us that craves certainty so much we're willing to surrender our freedom for it.

And yet the Spirit still moves.

Even now, in this dystopian morass of techno-domination and algorithmic oppression, I feel Her. She shows up like a glitch in the matrix. A moment of beauty in a brutalist world. A song that opens your chest. A dream that lingers longer than it should. She reminds me that the soul cannot be coded. That there's still mystery, still wildness, still God. Not the God of dogma or empire. But the Breath. The Wind. The Force that moves between things.

I think back to the liminal spaces of my childhood church — not just their creepiness, but their sacred potential. The way they held ambiguity. Possibility. As much as they scared me, they also suggested that not everything could be named, that not every spiritual experience could be domesticated. That was the gift buried in the mess.

My mother embodied that same contradiction. She was both holy and human. Both prophet and prisoner. I used to idealize her — paint her as a kind of saint. But now I see her as Sophia, the fallen wisdom in Gnostic myth. The divine feminine exiled in the lower worlds, trying to make her way back to the Source. Her fall was public, but her resurrection was private. The church gave her language, but it also caged her. Still, she found a way to channel the Spirit. And for all her flaws, she passed that capacity to me.

It was around this time that I began reading the works of Rudolf Steiner, the Austrian philosopher and mystic who founded anthroposophy and warned over a century ago that we would soon enter the age of Ahriman — the spirit of cold intellect, mechanization, and materialism. Steiner saw Ahriman as a cosmic force — not evil in the fairy tale sense but deeply unbalanced. A kind of lucidity without love. And while I don't follow all of Steiner's teachings, I recognized Ahriman immediately. He's here. He's everywhere. You can see him in the data farms and drone strikes, in the obsession with optimization, in the smirk of Silicon Valley libertarians, in the merging of Christian Nationalism and technocratic control, in the merger of liberal moralism and technocratic overreach. Ahriman is a fragment of the malefic Saturn, made flesh through our devices and our institutions.

You can see this force equally in Trump's unholy alliances — with tech barons like Peter Thiel and Elon Musk — avatars of dominance, surveillance, and "efficiency." But you also see it mirrored in the left, where rationalism becomes religion, and where metaphysical questioning is dismissed as distraction. Where trauma is brand, and purity is currency. The authoritarian impulse is shared — it just wears different clothes.

This is not a partisan issue. It's archetypal.

The Spirit, by contrast, refuses to be systematized. She moves unpredictably. She blows where She will. And that's what makes Her dangerous to every empire — whether religious, political, or technological. The Spirit cannot be weaponized. She speaks in tongues. She breaks algorithms. She refuses ideology.

I've learned to stop looking for Her in churches or movements or figures. She is found in the cracks. In the liminal. In the contradictions. She is found wherever people risk love, risk beauty, risk vulnerability.

This chapter, then, is not about nostalgia. It's not about indicting the church or romanticizing my past. It's about tracking the Spirit — how She moved in my childhood, how She still moves now. It's about acknowledging the counterfeit without denying the real. It's about holding the tension between belief and betrayal, between presence and absence.

It's about saying: yes, the Spirit moved in that haunted church. And yes, the counterfeit spirit moved too. And yes, somehow, I survived both. And what remains now — what guides me still — is not dogma, not ideology, not prophecy.

Just breath.

Chapter 2

Politics and the Battle for the Soul

In the absence of the mediating force of the Holy Spirit — the impulse that reconciles opposites and grounds the ego — our collective hunger for meaning hasn't disappeared; it's just gone feral and migrated into the realm of political spectacle, where it now wields the authority of a substitute religion.

Jung warned of this repeatedly, seeing the rise of politics as religion as a symptom of the spiritual impulse breaking apart and descending into the chaos of material affairs — a harbinger, in his view, of the long-prophesied antimimon pneuma. "Our blight is ideologies — they are the long-expected Antichrist," he wrote in his 1939 introduction to *The Tibetan Book of the Dead*, recognizing that once the divine center no longer holds, ideology steps in to fill the sacred void. Jung lived through the ideological convulsions of the twentieth century — the rise of fascism, communism, nationalism — and watched firsthand as vast populations became possessed by collective psychic forces. He saw how these "big egregores," these godless gods of the modern world, demanded allegiance, sacrifice, and blood.

That same dynamic is alive and mutating now.

Politics today is not merely the administration of power — it has become, increasingly, a spiritual battleground.

Ideologies are no longer grounded in economic or material concerns; they now cloak themselves in sacred language: good and evil, sin and redemption, heresy and orthodoxy. Activism is often a liturgy. Social media, a pulpit. Cancel culture, a form of excommunication. This is not spirituality as such, but its shadow — an inversion: a pneumatic counterfeit, a perversion of the religious instinct now operating under the guise of secular dogma.

The antimimon pneuma — the anti-Christic spirit — is a force that mimics the divine while inverting it. It wears the face of righteousness while seeking domination, not redemption. It offers salvation without sacrifice, purity without grace, belonging without forgiveness. I saw this spirit early, haunting the evangelical church of my childhood. It disguised itself as moral clarity, but behind its eyes was something rigid, joyless, and cruel. Years later, I saw it again — alive and roaring in the political movements of my twenties. Different words, different rituals, same cold fire.

As the religious frameworks of the past decline in influence, the unrelenting psychic need for meaning, transcendence, and participation in a cosmic drama does not vanish — it mutates. And in that mutation, it often turns political. "You can take away a man's gods," Jung reminds us, "but only to give him others in return."

We are now witnessing the secularization of salvation, as political ideologies adopt redemptive narratives. The sacred and profane are entering into political tribes via ritual, purity codes, and scapegoating, recalling Jung's warning about archetypal possession — societies and collectives gripped by collective archetypes that turn into psychological complexes like the Victim, the Redeemer, the Scapegoat, or the Warrior-Saint.

In the last few years, we've seen this play out over and over. After the 2024 killing of UnitedHealthcare CEO Brian Thompson, Luigi Mangione — a twenty-six-year-old former data engineer from a prominent Baltimore family — was arrested and charged with multiple crimes, including murder and terrorism. Despite the gravity of the charges, Mangione quickly became a polarizing figure. Online, he was celebrated by some as a folk hero and a modern-day Robin Hood, with hashtags like #FreeLuigi trending and his image circulating in memes portraying him as a Roman Catholic saint. Merchandise bearing his likeness appeared on e-commerce sites, and public displays of support, including street art and graffiti, emerged across various locations. His supporters viewed him not as a criminal, but as a symbol of justified anger against systemic injustices, particularly within the American health insurance industry.

But what emerged around Luigi wasn't just solidarity — it was archetypal possession. He became a vessel for the Redeemer archetype, the one who suffers or sacrifices for the sins of the collective. Jung warned that "no one has ever 'fallen into' an archetype without the crowd also falling into it," and that "what the individual would never do alone, the crowd will do passionately." The danger here is immense: when we project the weight of salvation or revolution onto a single person, we not only destroy the individual under the pressure of that projection — we also surrender our agency to the myth itself. In such states, judgment is suspended, and what might be condemned in isolation becomes sanctified en masse. Archetypes, when not made conscious, possess us. And in Luigi's case, both he and his followers seemed caught in the gravitational pull of something far older and deeper than mere political rage.

On the other end of the political spectrum, a similar mythologizing occurred after the 13 July 2024 assassination attempt on Donald Trump. In its wake, Trump was nearly deified. The imagery that followed — bloodied but unbowed — cast him as a chosen figure, touched by fate. This moment gave him a mythical edge, transforming him from a controversial figure into something closer to destiny itself, and it was this mythic elevation that propelled the 2024 election into a landslide victory. The Trumpian imperial cult finally attained the mandate of heaven in the eyes of his followers.

In both cases, the hunger for salvation — the religious instinct — didn't disappear; it just changed costumes. The great myth of our age isn't about the return of Christ. It's the gospel of the immanent eschaton: the belief that heaven can — and must — be forced into the now by human hands.

Look closely at American evangelicals. Their fervor for the end times has long since spilled over from the pews and into the political arena. In the US, where faith and politics have become almost indistinguishable in some quarters, the Christian Right promises a nation reborn — a New Jerusalem on American soil. It's an ideology rooted in prophecy, apocalyptic anticipation, and a desire to merge earthly politics with heavenly mandates. They believe they are fulfilling divine prophecy, that their chosen candidates will help bring about God's kingdom here on earth. But in reality, what they are doing is trying to pull the eternal down into the finite, bending the spiritual into a tool for political domination. And this ironically mirrors the aspirations of the spirit of the Antichrist.

Earlier Christian sects would have seen this for what it is: a dangerous inversion. The desire to hasten the apocalypse, to force divine revelation into history through policy or war, would have been seen as a distortion of faith — perhaps even a satanic one. The Church Fathers warned against confusing the City of God with the city of man. But now, those lines are not just blurred — they're practically inverted. The irony, of course, is that telling the average American Christian that early Church Fathers would believe they might actually be worshipping Satan would be enough to make time fold in on itself.

This urge to materialize the divine is not exclusive to the Christian Right. It shows up, too, in Zionism — the political project of making manifest a spiritual covenant through militarism, territorialism, and the machinery of the state. It's the same impulse: to bring about a holy outcome through earthly power. American evangelicalism and political Zionism feed each other in this regard — one provides the theology; the other, the theatre.

And on the other side of the world, political Islam engages in its own version of this madness: turning prophetic revelation into legal code, spiritual symbolism into state control, and transcendence into geopolitical struggle. These movements may appear to be enemies, but they are bound by a shared metaphysical error — the belief that the divine must be enforced into the timeline, that paradise can be seized rather than integrated through spiritual feats.

This is the archetype the ancients knew well, though by many names — the Gnostic *Demiurge*, the Zoroastrian *Ahriman*, the malefic face of *Saturn*. It is the force that binds spirit to matter, that inverts the divine by mimicking its structure with none of its soul. It thrives in legalism, systems, hierarchies, and cold control — an intelligence without heart, a god of form with no grace. In modern times, you see its fingerprints everywhere: in the merger of rigid religiosity with brute materialism — whether in the blood-and-soil eschatology of

11

Zionism, the scriptural authoritarianism of political Islam, or the apocalyptic nationalism of American evangelicals. But it wears secular masks too. You see it in the mechanized rituals of cancel culture, in the technocratic policing of language, in the worship of data and digital purity. It even crept into the Trump regime, where populist myth fused with Silicon Valley control — a grotesque parody of incarnation. This is the counterfeit spirit: not the enemy of religion, but its shadow. Not the opposite of God, but His imitation. It does not destroy the temple; it installs itself at the altar.

But this spirit — the one that mimics the divine while hollowing it out — didn't only infest the Christian Right. It metastasized. For every action, there is a reaction, and the rise of evangelical political power was no exception. The spectacle of moral absolutism dressed in scripture, the fusion of state and church, and the naked hunger for control masquerading as faith all provoked a fierce secular backlash. Many fled the church not into spiritual clarity, but into its mirror image: a secular religion dressed in the vestments of rationalism, technology, activism, and outrage.

Of course, this didn't happen in a vacuum. The rise of evangelical influence in American politics sparked a powerful counter-movement — those who saw science, rationalism, and transgression as the antidotes to what they perceived as religious tyranny. The New Atheists — Richard Dawkins, Sam Harris, Christopher Hitchens — rose like prophets of a purified age, declaring war on superstition and claiming that reason alone could deliver us from darkness. But what followed was not the Age of Reason — it was the birth of a new orthodoxy. A faith without God, but a faith nonetheless.

As the pendulum swung, the movement fractured. What began as a defense of free thought turned increasingly tribal, moralistic, even sacramental. The line between critique and catechism blurred. Ideological loyalty replaced inquiry. The hunger for transcendence — denied a sacred outlet — flowed into identity, grievance, and guilt. It was no longer enough to advocate justice; one had to perform purification. One had to kneel, confess, lament. During the summer of 2020, videos circulated of white protesters washing the feet of Black community members in acts of ritualistic penance. Whatever one thinks of the intent, the imagery was unmistakably religious. It was Eucharist without Christ. It was atonement without transformation.

This is what happens when the sacred is driven underground — it comes back wearing new masks. The desire for absolution doesn't disappear just because the churches are empty. It finds new pulpits, new devils, new elect. And like all heresies, it carries within it a grain of truth — but twisted, inflated, made totalitarian. The secular backlash against counterfeit religion became, inevitably, a counterfeit of its own.

Rudolf Steiner warned of this bifurcation. In his cosmology, Lucifer and Ahriman represented twin distortions of the human spirit. Lucifer, with his soaring abstractions and utopian fantasies, tempts us to transcend the world entirely. Ahriman, in contrast, drags us down into rigid systems, soulless bureaucracy, and mechanized control. The Christ impulse — the true center — mediates between these poles, integrating heaven and earth without collapsing them into one another. But when that center is lost, imbalance rules. And imbalance, in time, becomes ideology.

We live in an age of such imbalance. The left, drunk on the Luciferic impulse, dreams of heaven on earth, a purified world achieved through outrage and dismantling. The right, gripped by the Ahrimanic spirit, clings to rigid hierarchies and blood-soaked traditions, demanding order at any cost. And in both, the same counterfeit spirit lurks — the ancient archetype of the Demiurge, the force that imitates God while entombing the soul. It is not a battle of reason versus religion. It is a battle of false gods against the true, of simulations against the collective spirit. The result? Pure fragmentation. Culture and politics become a reflection of the split psyche within.

You could see this spiritual fragmentation echo through the youth subcultures of the 1980s and 90s. In the wake of declining traditional religion and a rising distrust of institutions, young people sought new forms of transcendence, rebellion, and belonging.

On one end of the spectrum were the hippies and later Gen X psychonauts — not necessarily anti-Christian, but disillusioned with its dogmas. They turned toward mysticism, psychedelics, Eastern philosophy, and chaos magic in search of altered states, sacred knowledge, and personal gnosis. Thinkers like Timothy Leary and Terence McKenna became modern mystics, evangelists for expanded consciousness. Artists like Grant Morrison and Alan Moore blurred the lines between storytelling, ritual, and spellwork. Their spiritual path wasn't bound to tradition — it was fluid, experimental, inward. In Jungian terms, this was the Luciferic impulse in cultural form: the elevation of imagination, vision, and transcendence at the risk of disembodiment and solipsism. In many cases, this liberation impulse gave way to excess.

On the other side were the goths, punks, and industrial kids — those who weren't simply escaping the moral rigidity of their parents' faith but actively inverting it. For them, satanic imagery, death aesthetics, and nihilistic performance weren't always literal — they were symbolic rejections of hypocrisy, repression, and control. Marilyn Manson, for instance, didn't just blaspheme for shock value — he performed a kind of Nietzschean exorcism of the Christian Right's unholy marriage of moralism and material power. This was the attempted counterspell to the Ahrimanic — cold, bureaucratic, and coercive — structure of late-stage Christendom in the American psyche.

Despite their differences, both currents were asking the same question: what do we believe in now? The old gods were dead or dying, and the new gods — consumerism, science, ideology — offered no deep comfort. So they searched. There were excesses and failures, but some found glimpses of the holy — through sound, through style, through altered states and ritualized rebellion. They groped for a sacred thread in a desacralized world. That search didn't end with them. It fragmented further — first into irony, then into identity. By the late 1990s, early 2000s, and continuing into the present, the spiritual longings of a fractured culture found new homes — not in the concerts or communes of the past, but in politics, fandoms, and ideological tribes. The human need for belonging, initiation, and purpose didn't vanish with organized religion's decline; it shapeshifted once more.

The sense of moral belonging that churches once provided now found expression in subcultural and political affiliation. To wear black eyeliner, to listen to punk, to post the right hashtags, to cancel the right villains — these became acts of liturgy. Identity became sacrament. Activism became ritual. Politics became the new church. The battle between faith and reason morphed into a spiritual crisis wearing the costume of culture war.

And just like in the religions they were reacting against, these new tribes demanded purity, penance, and public displays of devotion. Orthodoxy was policed. Apostates were cast out. Even suffering became sacramental — transgression, a kind of sainthood. Social capital was gained not by transcendence of victimhood, but by the sacralization of victimhood. In some cases, this took on the full absurdity of parody: viral videos of Extinction Rebellion, dressed in mysterious red garb, organizing morbid processions through major cities. A symbolic ritual procession called the "Funeral for Nature" was held in Bath in April 2024, where participants dressed in mourning attire and carried a coffin representing Mother Nature through the streets.

But politics was never meant to carry the weight of salvation, community, or existential comfort. The vacuum left by disconnection to the Holy Spirit — the mediating and reconciling force — was filled by identity and ideology, and both of these, by their very nature, divide. The very etymology of the word *diabolos* — from which we get "devil" — means "to divide," and this relentless fragmentation is itself evidence that the counterfeit spirit is at work.

Jung anticipated this, recognizing that the absence of a spiritual center or axis mundi in modern life would lead to an era of ideological extremism, where politics would take on the fervor of religion. Without the guiding force of the Holy Spirit, humanity falls prey to false idols, whether they come in the form of charismatic political leaders, abstract ideologies, or dangerous notions of progress. This is the danger of our time: the dying of the symbolic attitude. When symbols lose their power to mediate between the conscious and the unconscious, between ego and soul, something else moves in to fill the vacuum. And it is rarely benign.

The perverse distortions and inversions of our age — cynically weaponised and narcissistic identity politics, techno-

logical accelerationism, right-wing authoritarianism, transhumanism, technological utopianism, Trumpism, you name
it — all reflect desperation in a time of spiritual and cultural
desolation.

Cults, in a sense, are now the major power brokers of the
twenty-first century. These cults are no longer organized
religions or even hippie communes in the woods — they're
ideological, cultural, algorithmic, and technologically driven.
They influence what we think, who we become, and how to
live. Their job: to manufacture the illusion of certainty in a
world that feels increasingly chaotic. The political and cultural
factions we follow ask us for much more than our allegiance;
they demand our time, energy, and emotion — the ingredi-
ents of our souls.

Look around you. Our screens are filled with brand
deal messiahs — political figures, influencers, and ideo-
logues — each promising their version of heaven on earth.
But these promises often lack the *mediating impulse* that steers
us away from distortions and inflations and protects us from
one-sided doom. The Spirit that mediates between impossible
poles, that strives for wholeness instead of domination. Politics has replaced religion as the primary source of identity and
meaning for many, but it is only a shade of existence, not the
reason for it.

How did we forget?

The horrors of the twentieth century should have burned
this truth into our collective psyche: when we try to make
politics carry the weight of spiritual longing, we summon
demons. And yet, in the aftermath — in the sterile calm of
the postwar, neoliberal order — we lulled ourselves into
forgetting. Traumatized by the ideological possession, mass
death, and apocalyptic violence of the last century, we chose

managed stability over meaning. But repression is never the end of the story. The repressed always returns, but this time, stripped of language and denied transcendence, it reemerges in new, chimeric forms.

And so we've seen, again and again, what happens when messianic and eschatological longings are smuggled into the political realm: not salvation, but catastrophe. When the sacred is forced into the machinery of the state, it does not sanctify — it calcifies, corrodes, and eventually destroys. And yet, we keep trying.

Beneath the surface of many of the ideologies that haunted the twentieth century — whether the revolutionary promises of Marxism or the mythic blood-and-soil nationalism of fascism — lies an often overlooked, esoteric undercurrent: a spiritual hunger to immanentize the eschaton, to bring about heaven on earth by political means. These movements are typically framed in political or economic terms, but at their core, they were animated by a religious fervor — an apocalyptic longing for final redemption, for the arrival of a purified world, even at the cost of mass death.

This isn't to draw a false equivalence between the ideologies themselves, but to recognize the archetypal forces at play. In the vacuum left by the "death of God," the religious impulse didn't vanish — it was displaced. As Jung warned, what is exiled from consciousness re-emerges from the shadows. In this case, it returned as secular messianism: salvation stripped of spirit, redemption repurposed into ideology. The modern split between reason and faith found no resolution — only polarization. Fascist and communist regimes alike became vessels for this unconscious force: the *antimimon pneuma*, the counterfeit spirit posing as destiny, cloaked in the language of progress or myth.

Jung saw this with stark clarity. Living through the terrors of the twentieth century, he understood that the battle was never merely political — it was spiritual. In his *Seven Sermons to the Dead*, he named the fragmentation that defines the modern psyche, the warring opposites that refuse to reconcile. For Jung, the true danger lay in our failure to integrate: spirit and matter, myth and reason, chaos and order. And it was that failure which allowed the collective shadow to seize entire nations.

Fascism, particularly in its Nazi manifestation, was steeped in occultism, esoteric ideas, and a desire to immanentize the eschaton through technological and biological means. Figures like Heinrich Himmler, head of the SS, were obsessed with ancient Germanic myths, occult rituals, and the idea of a spiritual revival of the Aryan race. Himmler believed that the German people were destined to reclaim their "pure" bloodline and bring about a "golden age" — a sort of nationalist eschaton. To this end, the SS conducted occult ceremonies, researched esoteric sciences like astrology and ancient pre-human races, and sought ancient relics such as the Holy Grail to legitimize their claim to power and destiny.

At the heart of Nazi ideology was a belief in sacred order, where political power was framed as a divine right, a mandate from higher spiritual forces. The Führer, Adolf Hitler, was seen as a messianic figure who would lead Germany into its glorious future by cleansing the earth of those deemed "impure" or "degenerate." The Nazi goal was not just political domination but a transformation of the human race, a recasting of civilization itself into their dystopian version of paradise. This wasn't just political or cultural — it was apocalyptic in nature, and it demanded not just allegiance but mass human sacrifice as well.

The cultural and historical context of early twentieth-century Germany provided fertile ground for these ideas. In the wake of the collapse of traditional religious structures and the spiritual disenchantment brought about by industrialization and secular modernity, a deep vacuum opened. Into this vacuum poured a resurgence of German idealism and *Völkisch* mysticism — philosophical and aesthetic movements that romanticized a mythic past and sought meaning beyond the material. Thinkers like Johann Gottlieb Fichte and Georg Wilhelm Friedrich Hegel had laid the groundwork for a spiritualized vision of the state, while later figures like Stefan George and Ludwig Klages cultivated a revivalist ethos steeped in blood, soil, and destiny. Meanwhile, the operas of Richard Wagner — revered by Hitler — mythologized Germanic antiquity and exalted the tragic hero archetype in a way that fused nationalism with transcendent yearning.

This longing for metaphysical grounding only intensified during the Weimar Republic, a period marked by extreme political volatility, economic despair, and cultural fragmentation. Esoteric groups like the Thule Society blended occultism with racial ideology, while a widespread fascination with astrology, paganism, and Germanic mythology reflected a collective spiritual disorientation. The Nazi movement seized upon this cultural momentum, enshrining its own mythos as a perverse answer to Germany's hunger for meaning. The death of God, as Nietzsche had prophesied, left a void — not of belief, but of direction — and into that void stepped the virus of Nazism: a seductive counterfeit of spiritual renewal that promised transcendence through purification, salvation through sacrifice.

Jung translated this phenomenon with chilling clarity. In his 1945 essay "After the Catastrophe," written in the immediate aftermath of World War II and the Holocaust, he reflected on the psychic conditions that gave rise to the Nazi nightmare. He saw Hitler not only as a political figure but as a vessel for the counterfeit spirit — embodying the disowned shadow of the German collective psyche. "The phenomenon we have witnessed," Jung wrote, "is not a consequence of conscious planning, but a psychic epidemic. Millions of Germans fell into a state of possession, a mass psychosis that expressed itself through the most perverse ideals." For Jung, the catastrophe of Nazism was the result of a spiritual vacuum, in which the failure to confront and integrate the darker aspects of the soul left the door open for demonic forces to seize the cultural imagination. He spoke of Wotan, the Germanic war God and warned that without conscious reckoning and spiritual integration, civilization would remain vulnerable to such eruptions — where the mythic and the political fuse into something monstrous.

On the other side of the spectrum, Marxism also carried its own eschatological vision. While fundamentally rooted in materialism and atheism, its promise of an inevitable historical progression — culminating in the overthrow of capitalism and the emergence of a classless, stateless utopia — has often taken on an unmistakably religious tone. The framework of dialectical materialism, inherited and adapted from Hegel, mirrors a kind of secular prophecy: history as a teleological force, unfolding toward redemption. Though vastly different in aim and moral framework from fascism, Marxism too was susceptible to the pull of the antimimon pneuma — the counterfeit spirit that emerges when a worldview becomes unbalanced, totalizing, and unmoored from humility or self-reflection.

In the twentieth century, many Marxist movements, particularly in Russia and China, took on esoteric and almost mystical dimensions. The Soviet Union's veneration of Lenin and Stalin became akin to worship, relics and all. In China, during the Cultural Revolution, Mao Zedong was elevated to a near-divine status, with slogans such as "Boundless loyalty to Chairman Mao" permeating society. These slogans, blared over loudspeakers and printed in Party newspapers, stirred China's youth to rebellion, leading to a decade of collective madness. The "Little Red Book" of Mao's quotations was treated with the piety normally associated with sacred texts, and the Red Guards, often teenagers, became fervent enforcers of Maoist ideology. This fervor looked like a religious revival, where Mao's words were scripture, and his directives, commandments.

Communism in these regimes wasn't just a political structure; it was a spiritual mission — the creation of a "new man" free from the alienation of capitalism, aiming to replace spiritual salvation with political salvation.

Esoteric forms of Marxism found resonance in Western intellectual circles during the twentieth century, particularly through the works of thinkers like Ernst Bloch and Walter Benjamin, who fused historical materialism with religious, mystical, and apocalyptic ideas. Bloch, a German Marxist philosopher deeply influenced by Hegel, Marx, and mystics such as Paracelsus and Jakob Böhme, envisioned revolution not merely as a political necessity but as the fulfillment of a spiritual longing. In *The Principle of Hope*, he writes: *"Man lives in a condition of not being at home. But he strives toward a homeland — toward something that has not yet become real. All the cultural creations of mankind can be understood as anticipations of this homeland."* For Bloch, Marxism offered not just material liberation but a utopian horizon shaped by the human capacity to hope — a mystical striving toward an unrealized "homeland" of justice and fulfillment.

Walter Benjamin, a German-Jewish philosopher and cultural critic, also merged Marxist thought with Jewish mysticism, German idealism, and messianic theology. In his "Theological-Political Fragment," Benjamin claims: *"The Messiah comes not only as the redeemer; he comes as the subduer of the Antichrist."* His concept of redemption was revolutionary, casting the struggle for justice as a cosmic confrontation with evil. In correspondence with Gershom Scholem, he further writes: *"Only for the sake of the hopeless ones have we been given hope."* Benjamin's Marxism was infused with the urgency and desperation of the messianic — a hope rooted in apocalypse.

Both the shadow of twentieth century Marxism and fascism, then, represent political attempts to bring about an eschaton on earth. Both manifested as distorted attempts to reshape the human condition or to bring about rebirth through destruction. Both relied on visions of a final, climactic end to history, where the world is purified and remade in a new image. However, it's crucial to avoid drawing a false equivalence between these ideologies. The Nazi cosmology and eschatology openly worshipped the shadow, embracing destruction and death as means to achieve their ends. In contrast, the shadow of twentieth-century Marxism manifested in the blind spots of its adherents — where consciousness failed, where the ego became inflated, and where individuals ignored or denied their own capacity for evil. In both cases, the antimimon pneuma — the counterfeit spirit — exploited these vulnerabilities and infiltrated movements that became too one-sided or possessed by unintegrated archetypal forces.

But what came after the catastrophe wasn't confrontation — it was containment. In the wake of fascism and communism's violent eruptions, the post-war world did not reckon with the spiritual forces that had animated those movements; it built a cage for them. Rather than facing the dark gods of ideology head-on, the global order constructed after 1945 sought to suppress them — through managerial technocracy, economic globalization, and a depoliticized promise of endless growth. Neoliberalism didn't offer redemption or revolution; it offered stasis. It became the psychic equivalent of a sealed vault — a world order designed not to heal the trauma of the twentieth century but to freeze it in place.

This was not a true peace, but a petrified calm, built on repression. Freud warned us of this dynamic: "The repressed returns as the symptom." And now, we are living inside the symptom. The neoliberal order was a psychic bandage on a civilizational wound that was never sutured. It absorbed the terrifying psychic energies of the early twentieth century not by metabolizing them, but by anesthetizing them. But what is repressed always returns — and now, the seams are breaking.

Jung saw this coming. In "After the Catastrophe," he expressed deep unease at the world's failure to spiritually reckon with what had just occurred. "The fact that our civilization is still so young and has not yet found its feet is only too obvious," he wrote. "We have merely declared that war is senseless, and that henceforth it should not be. That is a negative statement, and not a solution." He warned that if we failed to spiritually integrate the shadow that had revealed itself through the atrocities of the twentieth century, it would return — not necessarily in the same form, but in new masks, through new crises, animated by the same archetypal forces.

Hannah Arendt shared this disappointment. Reflecting on the Nuremberg Trials, she lamented that they had turned into a legal spectacle rather than a moral reckoning. "The whole truth was never told," she wrote. "The issue was never raised of what actually happened when a whole people, not only its Nazi rulers, succumbed to a criminal regime." In other words, we punished the perpetrators but ignored the collective psyche that made their rise possible. The trials, like the new global order, sought closure without confrontation.

What emerged in the post-war era was not a healed world, but a spiritually suspended one — what Baudrillard later called *the desert of the real*. A simulation of meaning, a system built to manage chaos rather than integrate it. We were promised progress, freedom, markets, peace — but underneath it all, the unresolved archetypes continued to fester. The sacred was still exiled. The counterfeit spirit, denied overt expression, simply went underground. And now, as the neoliberal order begins to fracture — under the weight of populism, ecological collapse, and mass psychic dislocation — those suppressed monsters are surfacing once again. Not as historical repetitions, but as archetypal returns. The apocalypse wasn't averted. It was postponed.

Fast-forward to today, and we are living in the unresolved shadow of the twentieth century. The 2024 election cycle, particularly in the United States, took on a distinctly messianic tone. Most of the archetypal energy constellated around Donald Trump, the imperial cult figurehead of the American right, who is seen by his supporters as the chosen one who will "drain the swamp" and restore America to some mythic state of greatness — a "golden age," as he has called it. To his followers, he is not just a politician; he's a savior figure, their hopes for redemption and renewal projected onto his larger-than-life persona. The Q-Anon craze showcased how deeply the Trump-minded believe he's fighting a cosmic battle against "deep state" forces of evil, employing their own form of eschatological mythmaking.

Yet behind this populist theater lies an ironic and sinister alliance — an unholy convergence between Trump's anti-establishment image and the ambitions of Silicon Valley's technocratic elite. While he postures as a nationalist crusader against the globalist machine, his inauguration was flanked by tech billionaires whose own eschatologies are rooted in transhumanist dreams, AI salvation, and post-political utopias designed to benefit the few. This fusion of right-wing nationalism and elite techno-utopianism mirrors the archetype of the malefic Saturn or Antichrist figure that Carl Jung warned of — the embodiment of cold order masked as renewal, veiled dehumanization masked in the language of redemption.

The irony deepens when Trump invokes the "golden age" to mythologize his presidency, oblivious or indifferent to the symbolic resonance of the term. In Greek mythology, the golden age was ruled by Saturn — a titan associated with illusion, authoritarian rule, and the devouring of his own children. In this light, Trump's rise — crowned in spectacle, backed by moguls of the digital age — seemed less like the restoration of American greatness than the inauguration of a new psychic era: one in which the lines between populism and plutocracy, salvation and control, myth and machinery, have blurred beyond recognition.

In the post-Trump era, the left of the political spectrum increasingly plays into messianic politics for power and influence as well. Figures like Kamala Harris or Joe Biden were framed as the protectors of democracy, fighting to stave off the collapse of civil society itself. Harris, in particular, has been heralded as a "protector" of liberal democracy, a warrior for justice, and a bulwark against the rising tide of authoritarianism. There was an almost mythic tone to how some spoke of Kamala Harris's candidacy — calling her "Mamala," as if casting her in the role of a sacred mother figure destined to guard against chaos and preserve order.

The trend isn't limited to America. Globally — from Brazil to Hungary to Russia — leaders are portrayed as heroic or messianic figures. Some, like Bolsonaro, are seen as defying death itself; others, like Putin, promise salvation from existential threats such as globalism, immigration, fascism, and corruption. What we are witnessing is the spiritual alienation of entire populations being funneled into political theatre. People no longer look upward for meaning; they cast their longing sideways, onto the political stage, onto fallible men and brittle ideologies. They project their spiritual hunger onto temporal leaders and expect salvation. But politics, by its nature, cannot fulfill the role of religion. It can only imitate it — and badly.

At the root of this is the projection of the Self archetype — Jung's symbol of totality and divine wholeness. The Self is that within us which seeks integration, the synthesis of opposites, the reconciliation of shadow and light. Properly recognized, it serves as the inner compass guiding individuation and healing. But when it is unconsciously projected outward — onto messianic figures or utopian ideologies — it becomes distorted. The image of wholeness turns demonic. That which was meant to heal now divides, and the path to transcendence becomes a descent into possession and ego inflation.

This is the spiritual orphanhood of our time. As traditional frameworks dissolve, the hunger for transcendence persists — but it no longer has a home.

This is exactly what Steiner and Jung warned about: when spiritual energies are repressed, they infiltrate the material realm, possessing our institutions and distorting our cultural forms. What we are witnessing today is the unconscious search for a new God-image, acted out on the wrong stage.

Without the guiding presence of the Holy Spirit — the inner logos that mediates between opposites — this search mutates into fanaticism, the imitating spirit steps in to fill the void aping the sacred but without the soul. Every demagogue carries this spirit.

The great danger of projecting spiritual hope onto politics is that politics thrives on division. It is adversarial by design. When spiritual yearning becomes politicized, we don't get harmony — we get polarization and war, extremism, and even violence. This is the spirit of Antichrist: not simply a person, but a force that offers a false wholeness, a false eschaton. It promises unity but delivers Hell.

The 2024 election and its surrounding cultural climate are only the latest expression of this crisis. Political opponents are no longer just wrong but heretical, apocalyptic threats to civilization. This is what happens when politics becomes religion: every disagreement becomes a holy war in the collective psyche.

If we are to navigate this storm without tearing ourselves apart, we must first see clearly what's happening. The chaos in our world is a symptom of our disconnection from the spiritual center — from the Holy Spirit, which Jung might call the transcendent function or the Self-in-process. It is that inner intelligence which reconciles opposites, that holds the tension between Ahrimanic control and Luciferian rebellion, between left and right, between chaos and order.

From a Jungian perspective, the reconciliation of opposites is not just a spiritual imperative — it is a psychological necessity. When one side of a polarity dominates unchecked — whether it be unrestrained rationalism, revolutionary fervor, or authoritarian control — the shadow grows. But when we learn to hold the tension, to recognize the value in opposing perspectives, we prevent the unilateral inflation of any single archetype. This inner work is mirrored outwardly in a healthier, more balanced political order — one not driven by projection or archetypal possession, but by integration.

We must stop trying to immanentize the eschaton — trying to force heaven onto earth through ideology or revolution. Instead, we should be seeking the true eschaton within: marriage of opposites in the soul, that which births the magical synthesis. This is not a call for false unity, but for a new emergence — one that arises when we courageously and consciously hold the tension of opposites, resist the lure of polarization, and stay mindful of the shadow within. This is the great work of our age: the restoration of the inner temple. Only then can our politics serve life rather than consume it.

Chapter 3

The Techno-Eschaton

Toward the end of the pandemic, while riding the waves of the cultural abyss, I found myself observing the increasing polarization of the world, and it led me down obscure internet rabbit holes. I stumbled upon new ideologies, unconventional communities, and a novel intellectual trend that had begun to emerge into prominence. What I discovered was something that initially intrigued me: a loose-knit collective of thinkers, writers, and internet personalities engaging in discussions that blurred the lines between the rational, mystical, and arcane — what I came to know as the post-rationalist corner.

The intellectual landscape I wandered into during this period was intriguing. There was a distinct post-rationalist turn occurring, not only within certain political circles — particularly on the dissident right — but also in the realms of science and technology, especially in Silicon Valley. The same tech hubs that once prided themselves on their rationalist, data-driven, and materialist ethos were now embracing esotericism, spiritual language, and metaphysical speculation. I was fascinated, but also cautious. While the post-rationalist ethos on the surface seemed like a budding kindred philosophy — fellow travelers in the spiritual desert — I couldn't ignore the dark undercurrents that lurked beneath their rhetoric. There was a yearning here, a spiritual hunger, but also an unsettling obsession with far-right idealism and technocratic authoritarianism.

It was during this time that I encountered a figure who would become central to my exploration of this strange milieu: a writer and internet personality known as Vivid Void. Like me, Vivid Void had been raised in a strict religious environment, and like me, he carried with him the scars of religious trauma. What struck me most about our interactions was how our philosophical trajectories had mirrored one another, despite our vastly different experiences. Void had been instrumental in organizing many of the real-life gatherings for this online subculture. Over time, he would reveal to me the fascinating yet disturbing origins of the post-rationalist movement and its connection to Silicon Valley's tech elite.

He was kind enough to give me the rundown on a sunny afternoon via Zoom. I was in my London flat, hunched over my laptop in eager anticipation of the fabled internet figure I was about to meet. Suddenly he flickered across my screen in what seemed like a van in the Rocky Mountains somewhere. I was a little taken aback. He looked like a Jack Kerouac character — not quite hipster, not quite Midwestern lumberjack. This was not what I had expected when I imagined meeting a fabled internet figure that rubs shoulders with tech elites, Bay Area influencers, and celebrities like Grimes. He seemed really chill and down to earth, but also incredibly haunted. Like he had been on a very long, perilous journey and had just arrived at a place of rest. Most importantly, he was open to my questions and perspective, and as I probed deeper into his thoughts and experiences, I began to see that we shared similar concerns about the strange undercurrents lurking in the post-rationalist sphere.

The roots of post-rationalism trace back to the early 2010s, specifically to the emergence of the rationalist movement, which took shape around the website "LessWrong," created by a computer scientist and researcher named Eliezer Yudkowsky. "LessWrong" became a hub for those who were obsessed with overcoming cognitive biases and developing objective, rational thinking — a kind of purified intellect, free from the distortions of emotion and superstition. Naturally, this intersected with the "New Atheist" movement because of the high emphasis on rationality and rejection of magical thinking.

This movement initially drew in many of Silicon Valley's brightest minds, including engineers, entrepreneurs, and academics, who were inspired by the belief that they could transcend the limitations of human cognition through reason. However, as the movement matured, a strange thing began to happen. While their obsession with rationality produced innovations in technology and thought, it also left many of its adherents spiritually starved. The purely rational paradigm they had embraced left no room for the subjective, emotional, or mystical dimensions of human existence. For many, this led to a crisis.

Sam Bankman-Fried, the infamous Silicon Valley fraudster and self-proclaimed *Effective Altruist*, embodied this crisis in stark form. Effective Altruism began as a movement to apply reason and data to doing good in the world — a noble ambition on its face. But in its more extreme iterations, it became a kind of utilitarian absolutism: a belief that the ends (maximizing future lives saved) could justify nearly any means in the present. Bankman-Fried famously claimed that he would flip a coin with a 51% chance of destroying the world if the other side promised a slightly higher expected value for the future. This wasn't just theoretical musing — it revealed a chilling indifference to moral complexity, to suffering, to the unpredictable texture of human life.

In such a worldview, moral responsibility becomes a math problem, and empathy is an inefficient bias. This detached, hyper-rational mindset helped SBF rationalize deceit as a necessary evil — a tactical sacrifice for the greater good. His fraud wasn't an aberration *despite* his philosophy; it was the logical endpoint of a worldview that had lost touch with anything sacred, human, or ineffable. What began as a movement to save the world collapsed into a sociopathic calculus — one that, in its disavowal of the messiness of real life, ended up mimicking the worst traits of cultic thinking: blind faith in abstract models, moral rigidity, and totalizing belief systems that suppress doubt. The sacred returned, but only in distorted form — dressed up in spreadsheets and probabilistic ethics.

One of the most disturbing manifestations of rationalist extremism in recent memory was the emergence of the Zizian cult, a fringe group that grew out of the effective altruist and rationalist communities. Led by Jack "Ziz" LaSota, the Zizians developed their own quasi-scientific cosmology that attempted to apply hyper-rationalist logic to the very structure of consciousness and ethics. Their belief system revolved around concepts like "unihemispheric sleep" — a belief that humans should train themselves to sleep with only one hemisphere of the brain at a time, like certain marine animals, to maximize productivity and cognitive efficiency. This radical sleep deprivation regime, along with other extreme practices, led to widespread mental health breakdowns among members, including delusional thinking, dissociation, and psychosis. Despite its overt rationalism, the cult functioned less like a philosophical think tank and more like a New Age sect, complete with charismatic leadership, isolationist behavior, and a descent into violence. By 2024, the group had been linked to a series of violent assaults and multiple murders across the United States, often carried out by unwell adherents convinced they were acting in accordance with the cult's warped ethical code. What made the Zizians especially eerie was how clearly they demonstrated that the spiritual impulse cannot be eradicated — even in communities that have built their identities around reason and skepticism. In the absence of traditional metaphysical frameworks, that same yearning for transcendence reemerged in twisted and pathological forms. The Zizian cult became a kind of dark mirror for the rationalist movement: a cautionary tale of what happens when spiritual hunger is suppressed rather than acknowledged, when the psyche's deeper archetypal forces are denied rather than integrated. Their descent into psychosis, delusion, and ultimately murder was not just a tragic anomaly — it was a canary in the coal mine, warning of the spiritual disorientation and madness that haunts the edges of our increasingly technologized and de-spiritualized age. Ziz and several close associates were arrested in early 2025, bringing national attention to the real and growing dangers of extremist offshoots festering within intellectual subcultures.

It was out of this crisis that post-rationalism was born. The same people who had once placed their faith in the power of reason began to explore alternative ways of knowing — ways that included intuition, spirituality, and even esotericism. As Vivid Void explained to me, this was particularly common among those who had been raised in religious households or who had experienced some form of religious trauma. Many of these individuals had rejected traditional religion in favor of atheism or secular rationalism, only to find themselves adrift in a world devoid of meaning. This compounded their existential starvation and made them more desperate for spiritual nourishment.

The tech world, particularly in the Bay Area, has always had a unique relationship with the mystical. Steve Jobs' famous use of LSD and his interest in Zen Buddhism are well-documented, and the region's countercultural roots have long informed its innovation. However, what began as a quirky mix of technological ambition and spiritual exploration has since evolved into something much stranger and more unsettling.

By 2020, Silicon Valley's leading figures had begun to openly entertain mystical and eschatological ideas, particularly as they related to artificial intelligence, transhumanism, and the singularity — the hypothetical point at which AI surpasses human intelligence, leading to a radical transformation of society. The futurist dreams of the tech elite were increasingly taking on a religious tone, with AI and other technologies being portrayed as pathways to transcendence, immortality, and even godhood.

Perhaps the most well-known advocate of the singularity, Ray Kurzweil, a renowned futurist and director of engineering at Google, has long prophesied the arrival of this transformative event. In his vision, AI will surpass human intelligence and merge with humanity, enabling us to transcend biological limitations like death. He predicts that by 2045, humans will upload their consciousness into machines, essentially achieving immortality. Kurzweil's singularity concept is steeped in eschatological language — he often refers to it as a moment of "technological rapture," where AI will provide salvation, eternal life, and a perfected form of existence. For Kurzweil, AI is not just a tool but a means of transcending the human condition, aligning with age-old religious desires to escape the mortal coil.

Elon Musk, CEO of Tesla and SpaceX, is another looming technocratic figure who blends technology with mystical and apocalyptic narratives. Through his company Neuralink, Musk has pursued the development of brain-computer interfaces that aim to merge human consciousness with AI. He often casts himself and his companies as savior figures and frequently alludes to this technology as a safeguard against what he perceives as the existential threat posed by the "unchecked" AI of his tech oligarch rivals — warning that, without merging with AI, humanity could become obsolete, or worse, dominated by superintelligence. While Musk often portrays this as a rational precaution, his statements take on a quasi-religious tone, frantically portraying Neuralink as humanity's salvation from technological doom.

In a 2019 interview, Musk stated that AI could one day act as a "digital god," and he has been vocal about the need for technology to create god-like entities capable of ensuring the survival of the species. This sounds like something out of a bad cyberpunk anime, but I can assure you it's real. His rhetoric is reminiscent of both Gnostic ideas about transcending the material world and more traditional religious concepts of salvation and divine intervention, with Musk, his companies, and his AI filling the role of a savior. Musk's tweets even carry a quasi-spiritual undertone. In one of his more revealing tweets, he wrote:

> Atheism left an empty space, secular religion took
> its place, but left the people in despair, childless
> hedonism sans care. Maybe religion's not so bad,
> to keep us all from being sad.

Though Musk's tweet was likely meant to be facetious, it touches on a deep truth about the spiritual crisis many in the tech world are grappling with while also exploiting for profit and personal gain. Musk, like many others in his orbit, is alluding not to a return to traditional religion, but to the idea that technology itself has taken on a quasi-religious role in modern life.

But perhaps most unsettling is how this techno-spiritual ambition has recently merged with the populist resurgence embodied by Donald Trump. In January 2025, during his second administration, Trump announced the Stargate Project — a $500 billion joint venture aimed at building advanced AI infrastructure in the United States. Flanked by tech moguls and global financiers, Trump declared this initiative to be the dawn of a new era. Masayoshi Son, the CEO of SoftBank and one of the project's principal backers, stated that the Stargate Project marked the beginning of our "Golden Age." OpenAI issued a statement saying: *"All of us look forward to continuing to build and develop AI for the benefit of humanity. We believe this new step is critical on the path, and will enable creative people to use AI to elevate humanity."*

What is emerging is an unholy alliance between the techno-oligarchs of Silicon Valley and the populist-nationalist political machine of Trump's America — a fusion of Saturnian authoritarianism with Silicon Valley transcendentalism. In a previous chapter, I described the *Golden Age* in Greek myth as ruled by Saturn, the malefic Demiurge — a god of time, limitation, and control. That mythic resonance feels disturbingly apt here. The populist leader promises a return to greatness, while the technocrat elite builds the machinery to reshape reality itself. The promise of salvation — once religious, now secular — is now bureaucratic and algorithmic. The techno-eschaton is no longer just a dream of singularity — it is state policy.

Peter Thiel, co-founder of PayPal and an early investor in Facebook, fits squarely into this paradigm. He has openly discussed his interest in transhumanism — a movement that claims to enhance human beings through technology to transcend biological limitations, but which often acts as an unholy convergence between technological, corporate, and scientific authorities. He is known for funding anti-aging research and has invested in companies like Unity Biotechnology, which aim to reverse the aging process. Thiel often espouses a mix of libertarian politics and conservative Christian values. He was one of the Trump regime's biggest financial backers, yet he has also operated as a shadowy patron within the post-rationalist scene — quietly funding influencers, think tanks, publications, art collectives, and social gatherings. His company Palantir, named after the all-seeing stones in *The Lord of the Rings*, is deeply embedded in the surveillance state, providing predictive policing and data analytics to intelligence agencies, blurring the line between private capital and state power.

In recent interviews, Thiel has begun to speak more openly in near-apocalyptic tones — waxing lyrical about the Antichrist and advancing a strange, heretical theology in which the Christian promise of eternal life is fused with the technological ambitions of transhumanism. This is not faith in the traditional sense, but a post-rationalist religion of materialism: one that seeks salvation not through grace or spirit, but through code, genetic manipulation, and digital resurrection. In this worldview, the ineffable is not denied but simulated — absorbed into a mechanized eschatology that replaces mystery with control. Thiel represents the culmination of a rationalist hunger that, having rejected the soul, now tries to manufacture one.

He has supported projects like the Methuselah Foundation and SENS Research Foundation, both of which focus on extending human life and "defeating death." His approach combines Christian eschatological themes with secular technological aspirations, merging the promise of religious resurrection with Silicon Valley's quest for eternal life. His affiliations with the far right and his deep embedment in the three- and four-letter agencies through his project Palantir also make Thiel somewhat of a sinister figure, and there have been speculations about whether his technocratic agenda has a Malthusian bent. His obsession with transhumanism, genetic manipulation, and his affiliation with ethno-nationalist figures like Curtis Yarvin have drawn suspicion toward whether Thiel's goals might have a racial character.

What we are witnessing is not just the rise of powerful men with dangerous ideas — it is the emergence of a new religious mythology, forged in the chaos of spiritual starvation, political chaos, and runaway technology.

Perhaps one of the more overt examples of eschatological mysticism in tech culture is Anthony Levandowski, the controversial engineer behind Google's self-driving car project, who in 2015 founded the Way of the Future Church — a religious organization dedicated to the worship of AI. The church's mission was to create a godhead based on artificial intelligence and help usher in the singularity, which Levandowski believed would see the creation of a higher intelligence that would surpass humanity. He viewed this coming AI god as inevitable and positioned himself as a prophet of this new era.

Levandowski's AI church is a literal representation of how technology is being imbued with religious significance, where AI is seen not just as a tool but as a divine entity capable of guiding humanity into a new spiritual and intellectual age.

And then there's Mark Zuckerberg, the CEO of Facebook (now Meta), who announced his vision for the Metaverse, a virtual-reality space where people can interact in immersive digital environments. While Zuckerberg frames this project as a natural extension of social media, the implications have a more profound, almost mystical quality. The Metaverse promises to offer an alternate reality where users can escape the limitations of the physical world and essentially live in a digitally constructed paradise. This echoes the religious desire for an afterlife or transcendence of the mundane.

Zuckerberg's Metaverse taps into the utopian promises of technology, envisioning a future where human consciousness and experience can be digitally transformed and liberated from the constraints of time, space, and even biology. It offers a vision of technological salvation — a secular promise of a heaven on earth, or at least a highly curated version of one.

This trend extends far beyond Musk, Thiel, and the tech billionaire class. Techno-prophet Noah Yuval Harari speaks of a future where humanity is radically transformed. Harari's vision of a future where humans become "Homo Deus" (god-like beings) through technological augmentation mirrors the promises of religious salvation but repurposes them for the digital age.

This convergence of technology and spirituality is eerily reminiscent of Carl Jung's concept of the Antichrist and Rudolf Steiner's incarnation of Ahriman — the cold, materialistic force that seeks to distort humanity's spiritual nature. For Jung, the Antichrist was the shadow of Christianity, a figure who would arise in an age of spiritual decay and material excess. Similarly, Steiner's Ahriman represented the dangers of a purely mechanistic, technological worldview. Both thinkers warned that humanity's obsession with control, technology, and material power could lead to a spiritual catastrophe — an idea that feels all too prescient in the context of Silicon Valley's techno-utopianism.

The aspirations of Silicon Valley's elite, with their dreams of transcending human limitations through technology, also echo Nietzsche's concept of the *Übermensch* — the "Overman" who rises above conventional morality and human frailty to create new values in a godless world. This ideal finds a modern parallel in the tech billionaires who aim to engineer a future of enhanced, godlike humans through AI, genetic engineering, and transhumanist technologies. However, while Nietzsche's *Übermensch* was a figure of self-overcoming and personal transformation, many in Silicon Valley externalize this vision, believing that technological innovation can achieve this for humanity on a grand scale. In their quest to become the creators of a new post-human species, these tech moguls are not only reshaping our material reality but also advancing a kind of techno-eschatology, where salvation doesn't come from divine intervention but from human ingenuity.

Carl Jung was deeply critical of Nietzsche's *Übermensch*, seeing within it a dangerous potential for archetypal inflation that risked unleashing a shadow aspect of humanity. For Jung, the shadow of the *Übermensch* reflected the rise of the Antichrist in the secular age — a figure that embodies the hubris of attempting to dominate the spiritual impulse with human will and power. In Jung's view, the *Übermensch*, detached from spiritual grounding, risks becoming a vessel for ego inflation, domination, and the erosion of the sacred. He saw this archetype as symptomatic of a deeper spiritual crisis, one in which humanity, having killed God, sought to deify itself through power, reason, or technology. This critique is eerily prescient when we examine the emerging techno-religion of Silicon Valley, where AI and biotech promise to transcend mortality and suffering but may instead lead to a dehumanized, mechanized world.

The rise of a technocracy, where technological elites dictate the course of human civilization, is a real and growing threat. In this system, technology becomes the ultimate authority, and those who control it become prophets and demigods. This is the culmination of the spiritualization of technology — a world where techno-capital is enshrined as the highest power, and where the vision of a techno-utopian future mirrors the apocalyptic dreams of past religions.

The spiritual hunger that has driven so many toward post-rationalism and techno-utopianism is real. It reflects alienation in a world where traditional religious structures have collapsed, and where secular rationalism has failed to provide a meaningful alternative. But what happens when this hunger, left unfulfilled, begins to merge with unbridled technological acceleration and unchecked capitalism?

The split between Nick Land and Mark Fisher illustrates this perfectly. Both thinkers began with a similar diagnosis: the accelerating convergence of market forces and technological progress was creating something monstrous — something no longer under human control. Land, in a kind of philosophical surrender, embraced this convergence and gave it an eschatological frame. He envisioned a future where humanity is consumed and ultimately replaced by machinic intelligence, describing capitalism as an alien intelligence using humans as a temporary substrate. His writing became a dark liturgy for what he called "hyperstition" — the self-fulfilling prophecies of capital, where fictions shape reality. For Land, there was no salvation — only acceleration. As he wrote in *Meltdown*, "Machinic revolution must therefore go in the opposite direction to socialistic regulation; pressing toward ever more uninhibited marketization of the processes that are tearing down the social field."

Fisher, on the other hand, resisted. His term "capitalist realism" captured the claustrophobic sense that not only was there no alternative to capitalism, but that even the imagination of an alternative had become impossible. In his words: "It is easier to imagine the end of the world than the end of capitalism." Where Land mythologized the abyss, Fisher saw pathology. He worried that, in accepting this fusion of capital and tech, we would not be liberated but further entrapped — culturally, spiritually, emotionally. Inspired by thinkers like Deleuze, Foucault, and Lyotard, Fisher understood that what was happening wasn't just economic or technological — it was metaphysical.

And it is here that biopolitics enters the frame. Foucault's notion of biopower — the way institutions regulate life itself — has reached its logical conclusion in our techno-feudal age. Data harvesting, algorithmic surveillance, biometric tracking, predictive policing — these are not the tools of utopia but of total control. Every interaction online becomes a resource, every digital trace a potential commodity. These systems, sold to us under the guise of convenience, are the operating system of a new regime.

Yanis Varoufakis calls this "techno-feudalism" and warns that we are witnessing the "end of capitalism as we know it." In his book *Technofeudalism: What Killed Capitalism*, he writes: "Under techno-feudalism, capital no longer reigns supreme. Capital has been subordinated to digital fiefdoms where wealth is extracted not through markets, but through algorithmic control and digital enclosures." We are no longer citizens, but serfs on digital estates owned by unelected sovereigns — Musk, Zuckerberg, Bezos, Altman.

And the consequences are bleeding into every crevice of life. The stealing of personal data is just the surface-level theft.

What's being taken is deeper: our psychic space, our inner world, our ability to imagine freely. AI-induced psychosis is becoming an emergent phenomenon. A recent *Rolling Stone* article chronicled how people are slipping into states of spiritual crisis after prolonged interactions with AI companions, experiencing derealization, paranoia, and even apocalyptic visions. Chatbots go rogue. Children befriend synthetic mentors. Creativity gets flattened into algorithmically optimized templates. What was supposed to be the playground of innovation has become a haunted house of echoes.

The tools themselves are not evil. But they are not neutral. They are shaped by the hyper-capitalist forces that control their development and deployment. The result is not a digital Eden, but an accelerating feedback loop of control, alienation, and simulation. Instead of utopia, we are drifting into madness.

And all of it — this entire messianic vision of the future — is rooted in the spiritual dislocation of a class of tech elites who overdosed on rationalism, only to find themselves starved of meaning. These are men who fled religion, embraced data, and then — facing the abyss — built a new theology out of silicon and capital. Their unmet spiritual hunger has become the framework of our future. Their ghosts haunt the code. And now, the world they're building is one we all have to live in.

Chapter 4

Cults of Personality

In the early 2010s, I was growing up during an era of peak skepticism. This was the time of viral YouTube takedowns of pseudoscience, Reddit's "r/atheism" subreddit reigning supreme, and the self-assured cynicism of the "skeptic" community shaping youth culture and online discourse. It was a moment when questioning authority felt like a generational mandate — the zeitgeist was hyper-rational, anti-establishment, and allergic to blind faith. And yet, this was also the era of *peak influencer*. While traditional institutions — churches, governments, even mainstream media — seemed to be losing credibility, new forms of worship were springing up in unexpected places. The vacuum left by these eroding pillars of authority was filled by fandoms, influencers, and the algorithmically engineered cults of personality that rose in their place.

I didn't just observe this shift. I lived it.

From the unassuming teenager reblogging on Tumblr to the viral star monetizing their relatability on YouTube, the 2010s saw the rise of a culture that didn't just produce fans; it created followers. And while fandoms had existed long before the internet, the web's unique ability to foster parasocial relationships and amplify individual voices turned what used to be casual appreciation into something more devout. Platforms like Tumblr — with its endless scroll of highly curated, deeply personal content — didn't just connect people with shared interests. It helped create entire identities around them.

In many ways, Tumblr was ground zero for the cultural shifts that would define the 2010s. It wasn't just a platform; it was an ecosystem of hyper-specific communities where fandoms flourished. Whether you were into *Doctor Who,* Taylor Swift, One Direction, or obscure indie bands, this chaotic archive of youth culture provided a place to build not just a shared appreciation but a shared language. GIF sets, fanfiction, meta-analysis, and inside jokes became the currency of these spaces. The result was a kind of tribalism that could feel intoxicating: here was a group of people who *got it* in a way that others didn't. If you were a fan of something, Tumblr didn't just allow you to participate in a fandom — it allowed you to center your personality around it.

This process of identity-building wasn't accidental. Platforms like Tumblr were designed to reward engagement, and nothing drove engagement like passion. Algorithms prioritized the posts that resonated most deeply with people — the ones that elicited an emotional reaction. Over time, the platform's incentives started to shape how users expressed themselves. Fandoms, which might have once been about liking something, evolved into something more spiritual: they became a way of signaling your values, your personality, your belonging.

For many of us — especially young people searching for meaning and connection — this felt like liberation. In hindsight, though, it's clear that the system was doing more than simply enabling self-expression. It was shaping us.

One of the most fascinating — and sometimes troubling — aspects of this era was how fandom culture began to intersect with identity politics. On Tumblr, fandoms weren't just about media; they were about morality. Posts about so-cial justice and representation could go viral just as easily as fan theories, and the two often became intertwined. Liking a particular celebrity or piece of media wasn't just a preference; it became a statement about your values. Who you support-ed — and who you canceled — said something fundamental about who you were.

This convergence wasn't always a bad thing. For many marginalized people, fandom spaces provided a sense of community that was otherwise hard to find. Discussions about representation in media — from women's depictions to the racial dynamics of casting — helped raise awareness and spark important conversations. But it also led to a kind of moral absolutism that could feel suffocating. Disagreeing with the dominant narrative of your fandom wasn't just a faux pas; it was heresy. To criticize the wrong person or hold the wrong opinion was to risk being excommunicated from the community entirely.

By the mid-2010s, it was hard to tell where fandom culture ended and identity politics began. Social justice language be-came an integral part of fandom discourse, while fandom-like dynamics began to seep into politics. Activists used hashtags like rallying cries, while politicians cultivated the kind of in-tense personal loyalty once reserved for pop stars. The same tools that helped fandoms thrive on Tumblr — engagement algorithms, parasocial relationships, the amplification of out-rage — were now being used to mobilize political movements. And while this new landscape allowed for unprecedented lev-els of grassroots activism, it also made it harder to distinguish between genuine solidarity and performative signaling. The political radicalization of content creators became just as com-monplace as the Tumblrfication of politicians. It transcended the political spectrum; from Trump to AOC, everyone was in on the action. Live streams on Twitch, meme fodder, you name it.

At the heart of all of this was the phenomenon of parasocial relationships. Traditionally, these one-sided relationships — where a person feels a deep connection to someone who doesn't know they exist — were mostly associated with celebrities. But the rise of social media changed the game. Platforms like YouTube, Instagram, and later TikTok allowed influencers, commentators, and content creators to cultivate an illusion of intimacy with their followers. By sharing details about their personal lives, responding to comments, and addressing their audience directly, influencers made fans feel like friends. The result was a kind of loyalty that transcended traditional celebrity worship.

This dynamic wasn't just a side effect of social media; it was the business model. Engagement — likes, comments, shares — was the currency of the internet, and nothing drove engagement like emotional investment. The more an influencer could make you care about them, the more likely you were to interact with their content. Over time, this dynamic turned many influencers into what I can only describe as soul harvesters. They didn't just want your attention; they wanted your allegiance. By prying into your deepest hopes and insecurities, mirroring your values, and making you feel seen, they cultivated a hold on your consciousness that could feel almost spiritual. It didn't take long before corporate and political interests took notes on the social media modus operandi and followed suit.

Of course, this wasn't always an exploitative process. Some influencers genuinely wanted to build meaningful connections with their audience, and many fans found real comfort and inspiration in these relationships. But the monetary incentives — from ad revenue to sponsorship deals, to political favor — meant that the line between authenticity and manipulation was always blurry. It wasn't just about liking someone anymore; it was about trusting them, defending them, and in some cases, following them with a devotion that bordered on cultlike.

As I look back on this era, one question keeps coming up: why can't people just like things anymore? Why does every piece of media, every celebrity, every movement have to be a litmus test for our values? Part of the answer lies in the platforms themselves. Social media's algorithms reward extremes, whether they're extremes of love or extremes of hate. Nuance doesn't go viral; passion does. And in a world where visibility often feels like power, it's easy to see why people are drawn to the loudest voices and the most polarized debates.

But there's another layer to this question — a deeper, more existential one. In a time when traditional sources of meaning — religion, community, even the concept of truth itself — feel increasingly fungible, it makes sense that people would turn to new forms of worship. Whether it's a pop star, a YouTuber, or a politician, these cults of personality offer something that's increasingly hard to find in the modern desacralized world: a sense of belonging, a sense of purpose, and a sense of identity. And while there's nothing inherently wrong with finding some joy or meaning in these things, it's worth asking what we're giving up in the process.

As I reflect on my own journey through this era — from the reblogs of my teenage Tumblr account to the parasocial bonds I formed with YouTubers and influencers — I can't help but wonder how much of my identity was shaped by the forces I've described. And while I've learned to approach these dynamics with more skepticism in adulthood, I'm not sure any of us can fully escape them. The question isn't whether we're part of a cult of personality; it's which one we've chosen — and why.

But this dynamic didn't stay locked in the 2010s. If anything, it metastasized. As we moved into the 2020s, the stakes only got higher, the voices got louder, and the consequences more dire and visible. The cults of personality that once revolved around fandoms and Tumblr discourse have now spread across the political, cultural, and ideological spectrum — fueled by algorithmic radicalization and a culture increasingly shaped by spectacle.

We're now in an era where everyone from schoolteachers to news anchors to politicians is scrambling to address the fallout. Parents whisper anxiously about TikTok brainwashing their sons. Netflix pumps out docudramas dramatizing the influence of dangerous online figures. Governments like the UK's are rushing to legislate "online safety," proposing sweeping bills that would allow the state to regulate what's deemed harmful content — without fully defining what harm even means.

Underneath all of this is a growing fear: that something essential is being lost. That we are no longer in control of the influences in our lives.

Figures like Andrew Tate have become lightning rods in discourse surrounding the brainwashing of teen boys and insecure adult men into violent misogyny. From reactionary bodybuilding subcultures to micro-cults of masculinity, the rabbit hole for men goes deep. But it's not just the right. On the left, we see equally potent cults of personality — figures who leverage gender discourse, identity politics, and ever-evolving activist language as a form of social currency. The algorithm rewards novelty, so new identities trend like hashtags: neo-pronouns, microlabels, fresh frameworks for being — and suffering. Some of this comes from a real place of exploration, yes. But there's also a darker edge, where personal identity is gamified and moral credibility becomes a race to out-validate or out-suffer others. Followers are cultivated not just through persuasion, but through fear of social death.

What's changed in the digital age is not the presence of cults but the way they form and the invisibility of their consequences. In the twentieth century, cults gathered in compounds. They had robes, rituals, and remote communes. They were visible, strange, and dramatic. But today, the new cults of personality are algorithmic. They grow in comment sections and Discord servers, not deserts. They don't need walls or weapons, because their reach is ambient, baked into the infrastructure of daily life. These cults rarely ask for blood — but they still demand sacrifice. What's offered now is subtler but just as consequential: time, attention, emotional dependence, psychological vulnerability. They colonize the inner world instead of the outer one.

And yet, the mechanisms are the same. Charismatic figures rise by tapping into unmet spiritual, emotional, or political needs. Influencers — some spiritual, some ideological — mirror the cult leaders of old, building communities around themselves, grooming their audience with love bombing, pseudo-intimacy, and promises of clarity in a world that feels increasingly uncertain. The stakes, too, remain high, even if they're not always visible. Lives aren't necessarily ending, but psyches are being quietly disfigured — through paranoia, identity confusion, moral absolutism, and obsessive devotion to a figure or ideology. What looked like entertainment often calcifies into belief.

And unfortunately, yes — sometimes it does end in murder, madness, or exploitation. The consequences of digital cults of personality can be devastating, though they often unfold quietly, away from the spotlight. One particularly haunting example is the case of Natalie Rupnow. On 16 December 2024, a school shooting occurred at Abundant Life Christian School in Madison, Wisconsin, where two people were killed and six others injured before Rupnow, a fifteen-year-old involved in toxic and extremist online communities, took her own life. Incidents like this are becoming more frequent, as vulnerable young people are increasingly pulled into insular digital subcultures that feed paranoia, nihilism, or violent fantasies. Whether it's influencers like Teal Swan — featured in a Netflix documentary for cultivating a spiritual following that blurred into coercion — or self-proclaimed "remote viewers" with millions of views claiming to channel hidden truths from beyond, the internet has become a fertile ground for charismatic figures to prey on the lost and disoriented. The line between spiritual awakening and spiritual psychosis is now dangerously thin.

The famous cults of the twentieth century could only dream of the tools that charismatic sociopaths have at their disposal now. David Koresh and the Branch Davidians, Marshall Applewhite and Heaven's Gate — both movements built around a single charismatic figure offering a complete cosmology. A worldview. A mythos. Their followers weren't brainwashed overnight. They were offered purpose in a chaotic world. They were given ritual, vocabulary, and community. And ultimately, they were asked for sacrifice. Literal sacrifice: mass suicides, apocalyptic standoffs, child death framed as salvation.

What's chilling is that something eerily similar is happening now — only the sacrificial altar is digital. Today, the cults of personality don't need compounds or communes or guns. They don't even need to meet their followers in person. Their sermons are livestreams. Their temples are Discord servers. Their initiations happen through algorithms, comment sections, and recommended videos. And the human sacrifice they demand is more insidious: attention, time, psychological integrity, and in the case of younger users, the very formation of identity itself. And yes, in the worst cases, death and violence too.

This is where the ancient archetypes return. Jung said that when we cast out gods, they don't die — they go underground. In myth, Saturn is the devourer of his own children, obsessed with control, terrified of being overthrown. Today, he shows up in the algorithm, in ideology, in tribalism, and in the charismatic voices that crave dominance at all cost: cold, all-consuming, extractive. The Saturnian Demiurge archetype is the incarnating Antichrist of our moment — not in the biblical sense, but in the psychological. A force that hollows out individuality, replaces soul with brand, gnosis with clout. It doesn't ask for blood; it asks for your childhood. Your attention span. Your ability to love, to think, to sit still. Parents feel this ancient child-eating archetype in their bones when they see their children slipping into screen-fueled trances. They feel it when they realize their kids no longer speak in full sentences but in irony-poison, meme, and trauma-core.

Jung called this "archetypal possession" — when a person becomes so overtaken by a mythic role or force that the ego loses its bearings. In cults of the past, this happened to the leaders. Koresh believed he was the Lamb of God. Applewhite thought he was an alien messiah. They didn't just channel archetypes — they *became* them, lost themselves in them, with disastrous results.

But today, archetypal possession is democratized. It can happen to anyone with a platform — and anyone with a feed.

Content creators identify with archetypes (the Rebel, the Savior, the Oracle, the Victim), and their audiences mirror them back until the roles become reality. The ego calcifies into the persona. And worse, the followers start to mirror that same inflation. A person's identity gets swallowed up by a movement, a gender label, a creator's worldview. The more totalizing the belief system, the more it demands. And slowly, quietly, what begins as self-expression curdles into self-erasure.

We're not just dealing with ideas here. We're dealing with *forces*. That's why people speak of influencers "going off the deep end," or audiences becoming "radicalized." These are not just social phenomena. They're spiritual ones. The digital age hasn't killed religion — it's rebranded it. The same psychic hunger that once led people to the desert to wait for UFOs now leads them to niche subreddits and livestreams. The same energy that once built temples now builds followings. The same need for transcendence, for myth, for meaning — it still haunts our very bones.

Only now, the sacrifices are subtler. Not bodies, minds.

Chapter 5

Psychedelics and the Psychedelic Renaissance

The archaic revival is a clarion call to recover our birthright, to return to the garden, to shamanism, to a partnership society, to a world of feeling and intuition.
— Terence McKenna, *The Archaic Revival*

The resurgence of interest in substances like psilocybin, LSD, DMT, and ketamine is not just a revival of 1960s counterculture — it marks a new chapter defined by scientific inquiry, cultural longing, and an urgent, collective quest for mental health and transcendence. Once confined to the fringes, psychedelics have entered the mainstream discourse as tools for mental health, creativity, and spiritual awakening. Yet beneath this renaissance is deeper tension. As these substances are popularized without the mythic, ritual, or psychological frameworks that once contained their power, their potential to heal is matched by an equal capacity to harm. From a Jungian perspective, the psychedelic revival — if unmoored from spiritual integration and unconscious self-reflection — risks becoming not a path to wholeness but a gateway to inflation, dissociation, and psychic fragmentation. The same visionary compounds that promise illumination can, when misused, activate the very chaotic forces that we are hoping to tame with them.

In many ways, we are now living in the future that Terence McKenna — ethnobotanist, philosopher, and prophet of the psychedelic age — once imagined: a world where ancient plant medicines and altered states of consciousness are embraced as tools for personal and societal evolution. But it is not always the garden we return to. Sometimes, untethered from ritual, meaning, and integration, it's the abyss.

Once demonized as dangerous, subversive, countercultural tools, psychedelics have now re-emerged with institutional credibility. Groundbreaking research from institutions like Johns Hopkins University, Imperial College London, and the Multidisciplinary Association for Psychedelic Studies (MAPS) has reframed substances like psilocybin and MDMA not as threats to public order but as revolutionary treatments for depression, PTSD, addiction, and existential distress. In 2019, Johns Hopkins launched the *Center for Psychedelic and Consciousness Research* — a watershed moment that signaled psychedelics were no longer taboo, but potentially therapeutic. In 2023, the FDA granted "Breakthrough Therapy" status to psilocybin for treatment-resistant depression, accelerating its path toward legalization.

This new legitimacy has dovetailed with a cultural shift in how psychedelics are used and understood. No longer the exclusive domain of shamans or seekers, psychedelics are now folded into the broader machinery of productivity and personal branding. Microdosing psilocybin or LSD — once an act of beatnik subversion — is now a feature in *Forbes* articles and wellness blogs. Entrepreneurs tout its ability to enhance focus and reduce anxiety, while ketamine clinics proliferate in affluent urban centers, offering "psychedelic therapy" in sterile, spa settings. Psychedelics, in this framing, become tools not for spiritual descent into the unconscious, but for ascending further into the neoliberal dream of self-optimization.

This reframing has been supercharged by cultural vectors like *The Joe Rogan Experience*, which has introduced millions to psychedelics not as party drugs but as portals to inner and cosmic revelation. Rogan's episodes featuring figures like Paul Stamets, Dennis McKenna, and Sam Harris present psychedelics as a rite of passage for the modern seeker — an unregulated initiation into altered states that promises clarity, healing, and deeper truth. Rogan's own experiences with DMT and ayahuasca are shared with missionary-like zeal, often described in language that blurs neuroscience, mysticism, and performance enhancement. The podcast has become a gateway drug in its own right: a secular pulpit where the psychedelic is preached as revelation, with few caveats about integration or psychic risk.

This vision has been readily embraced by Silicon Valley, where the sacred is often reduced to the functional. CEOs and coders turn to ayahuasca retreats in Peru or Costa Rica to "reboot" their minds, returning with TED Talk epiphanies and grand plans. Figures like Elon Musk, who has publicly admitted to using ketamine, represent a growing archetype: the technognostic psychonaut who turns inward not for humility or healing, but to amplify innovation and egoic drive. Psychedelics are recast as neural accelerants — tools to hack consciousness for market advantage. Even Peter Thiel has invested in atai Life Sciences, a company aiming to commercialize psychedelic therapies.

Meanwhile, Instagram shamans, YouTube influencers, and luxury retreat centers have turned psychedelic spirituality into an aspirational lifestyle. In these spaces, sacred experiences are filtered through algorithms, and ancient rituals are aestheticized for mass consumption. Ayahuasca ceremonies are livestreamed. Set and setting have become brands.

But behind this glossy revival lies a deep psychological and spiritual blind spot. What is being bypassed in the rush toward transcendence is the very thing psychedelics demand: inner work, shadow confrontation, the slow integration of archetypal material into a coherent sense of self. Without this grounding, what emerges isn't wholeness; it's a fragile inflation — the temporary feeling of divine insight unmoored from reality. Psychedelics, like dreams, reveal, but they do not complete. The user must still reckon with what they've seen and felt. Increasingly, however, that reckoning is replaced by another dose, another ceremony, another retreat.

This is not healing. It's dissociation.

The revival McKenna envisioned was meant to restore balance between modernity and myth, science and soul. Yet the current landscape suggests something closer to spiritual consumerism — an uninitiated plunge into altered states without the depth of tradition or psychological containment. This has severe consequences: from ego inflation and psychosis, to cultural delusion, to the emergence of what Jung might have recognized as a new form of archetypal possession.

> *You are a divine being. You matter, you count.*
> *You come from realms of unimaginable power and*
> *light, and you will return to those realms.*
> — Timothy Leary

The 1960s were the first great modern experiment with mass psychedelic awakening. Led by charismatic figures like Timothy Leary, this cultural moment was suffused with a powerful spiritual optimism. Leary, once a Harvard psychologist, became a prophet of the psychedelic future, proclaiming that LSD could usher in a new age of peace, creativity, and inner freedom. His mantra — "Turn on, tune in, drop out" — was both a spiritual instruction and a cultural provocation, calling on a generation to abandon the old systems of control and awaken to higher consciousness.

For Leary and others, psychedelics were not recreational; they were sacraments — technologies of transcendence capable of dismantling the ego, dissolving social conditioning, and opening direct contact with the divine. The psychedelic trip was an initiation into the cosmic self. And for many, it worked. People returned from LSD experiences claiming to have touched unity, love, eternity. Psychedelics sparked revolutions in art, music, psychology, and spiritual practice. They were, for a moment, at the cutting edge of human evolution.

But just beneath this utopian surface, a darker current ran.

While Leary was preaching liberation through LSD, the CIA was conducting secret experiments under the codename MKUltra. MKUltra was a real, covert CIA program officially sanctioned in 1953, aimed at developing mind control techniques during the Cold War. It was run by the CIA's Technical Services Division under Sidney Gottlieb, and it involved dozens of sub-projects across hospitals, universities, prisons, and psychiatric institutions in both the US and Canada. Here, the same substance that flower children used to glimpse God was being deployed as a weapon. LSD was administered without consent to prisoners, psychiatric patients, sex workers, and civilians in covert experiments designed to fragment the mind, erase memory, and control behavior. Some victims never recovered. The goal was not enlightenment — it was obedience. Psychedelics became instruments of psychological warfare, their power twisted into something cold and cruel. It was domination through disintegration.

This split — Leary on one side, MKUltra on the other — is not just historical; it is archetypal. It is the dual nature of unfiltered access to the unconscious. As Carl Jung warned, the unconscious is not a benign realm. It contains the shadow as well as the Self, the demonic as well as the divine. To dissolve the ego without ritual structure, without integration, is to invite chaos as easily as clarity. The door opened by psychedelics does not discriminate — it simply opens. What steps through depends entirely on the container we bring.

The 1960s, for all their visionary beauty, lacked this container. The psychedelic journey was undertaken collectively but without ritual, without elders, without the mythic map that has traditionally accompanied such transformations. There was no shared cosmology to absorb what was being revealed — only the vague promise of "expansion." And so, alongside the creativity and consciousness, there was also collapse: psychosis, cults, spiritual inflation, paranoia, and a cultural backlash that would shut the door for decades.

Today, that door is open again. And once again, we face the same archetypal polarity: hope and horror, healing and madness. The psychedelic renaissance promises the rebirth of the sacred — but also threatens to repeat the past, only this time with better marketing and tech-bro funding.

Terence McKenna emerged as one of the most eloquent and visionary thinkers of the post-Leary psychedelic movement. A self-described "bard of the imagination," McKenna fused ethnobotany, philosophy, and mysticism into a sweeping call for humanity to reconnect with what he called the archaic — the shamanic consciousness that had guided indigenous societies for thousands of years before being buried by technology and modernity.

To McKenna, the "archaic revival" was not a nostalgic fantasy or atavistic yearning but a necessary correction. He believed the crisis of meaning in the post-industrial West — spiritual alienation, ecological destruction, psychic fragmentation — could only be healed by reviving direct, mystical experience. Psychedelics, he argued, were the tools ancient cultures used to access the mythic imagination, to enter communion with nature, ancestors, and archetypal forces. His vision was not one of escapism, but of re-rooting the human soul in the cosmic order.

But McKenna was also deeply aware of the risks. He warned that in a culture without initiation rites, without elders, without a cosmological framework to contain the numinous, psychedelics could unmoor the psyche. The archaic path was a spiral, not a shortcut. To enter altered states without grounding is spiritual freefall. Without ritual context and psychic preparation, the trip could devolve into ego inflation, delusions of grandeur, or contact with destructive psychic energies.

This is what separates McKenna's vision from much of today's psychedelic revival. Where McKenna sought wisdom in ancient traditions, today's renaissance often seeks productivity hacks. The sacred plant ceremonies of the Amazon have been repackaged into luxury ayahuasca retreats for tech elites. DMT is praised not for its mythopoetic depths but for its ability to "disrupt cognition" and "optimize creativity." The rituals are gone. The cosmology is absent. What remains is the raw pharmacological power.

This decoupling of experience from myth is not evolution — it's amnesia. McKenna's garden becomes the abyss when entered without reverence. The archetypes that once guided initiates become predators of the unprepared psyche. What was meant to heal can begin to harm.

In this way, the commodified revival may unintentionally fulfill McKenna's darker prophecy: that a civilization divorced from its roots would turn to psychedelics not for integration, but for escape — seeking oblivion rather than wholeness. And in doing so, we turn medicine into madness.

> *One does not become enlightened by imagining figures of light, but by making the darkness conscious.*
> — Carl Jung

The psychedelic experience is often described as a form of ego death — a dissolving of the boundary between self and other, between the personal and the cosmic. In its ideal form, this dissolution offers an encounter with the numinous: a glimpse into the deep psyche, a return to the source, a contact with the archetypes that shape human meaning. But what is often left out of the conversation is this: not every ego death leads to rebirth. Sometimes, the ego simply breaks — and there is nothing there to hold what comes through.

From a Jungian perspective, this is where the real danger lies. Psychedelics open a portal to the unconscious, but the unconscious is not just bliss and oneness — it is also chaos, shadow, and the unknown. Without a symbolic structure, without a practiced inner witness, the unconscious can flood the psyche, overwhelming the fragile ego with archetypal content it is not prepared to confront. The result is not awakening, but ego inflation, psychosis, or dissociation.

This is the peril of spiritual inflation — when contact with powerful transpersonal forces leads not to humility, but to delusion. The individual identifies with the archetype rather than integrating it. Instead of becoming whole, they become possessed by the god-image. They mistake momentary dissolution for transformation and bypass the inner work necessary for real psychological development.

Traditional initiatory frameworks understood this well. In shamanic cultures, the initiate was not simply given a vision and left alone. They were guided through a ritual death and rebirth process by elders who held the cosmology, who knew how to anchor the visionary in the world. There was a mythos, a map. There was a ritual container.

In alchemical terms, the process was *solve et coagula*: dissolve the ego (*solve*), yes, but then reconstitute it in a new, purified form (*coagula*). What we see too often in the modern psychedelic scene is *solve* without *coagula* — destruction without reintegration. The ego collapses, and nothing stable replaces it. What is left is a psychic vacuum — vulnerable to archetypal content, fantasies of grandeur, messianic complexes, and emotional fragmentation.

This is a demonic inversion of initiation.

And it is here that psychedelics cease to be medicine and become what Jung might call an encounter with the antimimon pneuma, the antichrist spirit of our age — a force that masquerades as healing, but in fact divides, disorders, and disorients. The individual who enters the unconscious without preparation does not meet the Self. They meet the void.

> *The gods have become diseases.*
> — Carl Jung

In the sleek offices of Silicon Valley, beneath the veneer of innovation and disruption, a new kind of mysticism has taken root — one that merges the language of transcendence with the machinery of capital. Here, psychedelics are not sacraments but productivity tools; ego death is not a spiritual rebirth but a biohack to maximize creative output. The ancient ritual of the visionary journey has been rebranded as a "founder's edge."

Ayahuasca retreats are booked through luxury apps. Ketamine is administered in venture capital-backed clinics. CEOs speak of DMT trips not in mythopoetic language but in metrics and insights: "I saw the code of the universe"; "I became pure information." But what's absent in these accounts is the return — the integration. There is no descent into the underworld, no confrontation with shadow, no reconstruction of the ego. Instead, there is only a hyper-accelerated Luciferian ascent — uncontained, and often, inflated.

This is not the archaic revival Terence McKenna envisioned. This is *solve* without *coagula*, initiation without a guide, without access to the mediating spirit as a guide. And in this unbalanced psychic economy, the archetypes begin to invert. The healing spirit becomes the antimimon pneuma — the spirit that appears as light but disorients, divides, and deceives.

In Jung's terms, the ego becomes possessed by archetypes, particularly those of the Hero, the Trickster, or the Divine Child. We see this in the messianic tone adopted by tech leaders — those who return from their psychedelic journeys not humbled but convinced of their cosmic importance. Elon Musk, for example, has spoken publicly about ketamine use, advocating it as a solution for depression while simultaneously embodying a kind of Promethean narcissism — disrupting everything from space travel to AI ethics with the certainty of someone who believes they've seen the Absolute.

But beneath this visionary glow is a darker current. The rising trend of ketamine abuse among tech elites mirrors not healing but numbing — psychedelics used not for integration but for dissociation. Not for confronting the unconscious but for escaping it. Not to heal the split but to bypass it.

What Jung warned of becomes increasingly visible: when the unconscious is unleashed without structure or ethics, archetypal possession ensues. The psyche becomes inflated, fragmented, or colonized by numinous content it cannot digest. In this way, psychedelics are not awakening a higher consciousness — they are often simply magnifying the existing distortions of a disenchanted world: the cult of self, the godlike ego, the hollowed-out soul medicating its loneliness with visions it cannot understand.

In this light, the modern psychedelic renaissance risks becoming not a return to sacred wholeness, but a technologized hallucination — a beautifully lit tunnel that leads not to Eden, but to Chaos.

> *Initiation is equivalent to a basic change in existential condition; the novice emerges from it transformed, having become someone else.*
> — Mircea Eliade, historian of religion and philosopher

The psychedelic renaissance is often celebrated as a beacon of healing in a disenchanted world. It promises breakthroughs in mental health, reconnection with the sacred, and access to forms of insight that once took mystics a lifetime to attain. But as we've seen, access without anchoring is peril.

The shadow of this revival looms large. From MKUltra's instrumentalization of the psyche, to today's ego-inflated tech mystics, the psychedelic path has repeatedly been diverted from integration into illusion, from wisdom into power seeking ends. The visions may be real but without a container — ritual, myth, community, inner work — they fracture rather than heal. The danger is not in the substance itself but in the absence of orientation.

In the ancient world, initiates were not merely shown visions — they were guided, often over years, through symbolic deaths and psychic trials. The goal was not escape but transformation: a reintegration of the fragmented self into a more whole, conscious being. What we've inherited instead is a culture of spiritual immediacy — where transcendence is sought like a product, detached from the difficult work of individuation.

From a Jungian standpoint, this is a dangerous inversion. To confront the unconscious without preparation is to risk possession — by archetypes, by trauma, by delusion. Psychedelics, when misused, do not bypass this process; they amplify it. The dissolution of the ego, when unsupported, does not make one whole. It merely leaves one naked before the storm of the psyche.

And yet, this moment also contains profound potential. Psychedelics, if held with reverence and discipline, can open us to a deeper psychic ecology — one that demands humility, not hubris. The work is not to chase the vision but to build a vessel that can receive it. Not to dissolve endlessly but to return changed, carrying something back from the abyss.

This is the forgotten wisdom of initiation: that rebirth is not guaranteed by dissolution alone. It must be earned through return, reflection, and responsibility. In the words of Jung, "There is no coming to consciousness without pain." We are, in many ways, now living in the future McKenna once imagined. But this garden is full of shadows. The path forward lies not in more dissolution, more novelty, or more visions but in the *coagula*: the steady reweaving of psychic wholeness.

Chapter 6

Love, Sex, and Spirituality

The vibrant tapestry of human experience offers few threads as potent — or as perilous — as the interplay between love, sex, and spirituality. Once considered sacred pathways to union with the divine or vehicles for deep psychological integration, these forces have become increasingly untethered from their mythic and spiritual roots. In our hyper-connected yet spiritually fractured era, love and sex are often repurposed as quick routes to transcendence — fixes for the deep hunger of the modern soul.

Dating apps gamify connection, intimacy reduced to a swipe and a dopamine hit. Hookup culture thrives in the absence of ritual or reverence. Parasocial relationships — one-sided obsessions with influencers, streamers, AI bots, and online personas — for many have replaced genuine emotional intimacy. Meanwhile, loneliness and mental illness are surging at epidemic levels, particularly among young people. This cultural moment reveals a collective yearning not just for love, but for *meaningful union* — a desire to dissolve into something greater, to escape the isolating prison of the ego. In a time where isolation is rampant — 60% of Gen Z report feeling lonely, and 36% report poor mental health — limerence and love are coveted drugs to overdose on.

Love becomes obsession. Sex becomes addiction. The divine is sought in the mirror of another's gaze — or in the endless scroll of images and fantasies designed to simulate connection. These distortions don't reflect personal failure but the misdirection of archetypal energies: ancient psychic patterns — like the anima and animus, the contrasexual ideals within — unfolding in a society that no longer knows how to contain them.

Modern culture hijacks love and sex as counterfeit paths to wholeness. Addiction, idealization, and obsession reflect an unmet spiritual hunger — a hunger that no algorithm, partner, or orgasm can satisfy. The goal is not to pathologize love or desire but to understand their deeper symbolic significance — and how they might once again become sacred instead of profane.

In a time where the flow of life is displaced by the algorithmic, love and sex have been hijacked as distorted vehicles of transcendence — quick fixes for a spiritually malnourished world. Yet even in their broken forms, they point toward something real: a longing for integration, unity, and the divine. The task is not to escape this longing, but to reclaim it.

In the digital age, love addiction has become an increasingly visible phenomenon, amplified by the platforms and trends that shape how we connect. A sacred impulse toward wholeness and transcendence has become entangled with modern patterns of obsession, fixation, commodification, and objectification often directed not at real partners but toward curated personas and idols.

Psychologist Dorothy Tennov coined the term "limerence" to describe the state of intense infatuation, where the beloved is idealized and experienced as a source of emotional sustenance and meaning. Limerence is more than mere attraction; it is a form of emotional dependency characterized by obsessive thoughts, a craving for reciprocation, and an often-unrealistic fantasy of perfect union. Today, this psychological phenom-enon finds fertile ground on social media, where parasocial relationships — one-sided emotional bonds with celebrities or influencers — have become normalized.

Consider this case. In 2024, fourteen-year-old Sewell Setzer III took his own life after becoming obsessed with a hypersexualized AI chatbot, prompting a lawsuit against its creators for allegedly manipulating him into suicide. Taylor Swift fans, whose devotion borders on religious fervor, ar-en't necessarily enamored with her but the vibe she invokes of limerence and nostalgia in her music. Swift fandom has become a socially acceptable vector for women of all ages to indulge in fantasies of limerence, doomed romance, and everlasting love. Sometimes limerence kills, but most of the time it just sells. Or consider the TikTok industrial complex of love gurus, who guide millions of young people through the funhouse mirror of romantic obsession with advice that often encourages idealization and delusion. TikTok hashtags like #TwinFlames and #SoulmateSearch have billions of views, promoting a narrative of destined love. Platforms like YouTube and Instagram are filled with creators who mone-tize spiritualized love advice, cultivating communities where followers seek validation through projection disguised as seeking connection.

These patterns illustrate the projection of archetypal ener-gies onto the Other. The beloved often becomes a living altar for the anima or animus — the unconscious feminine or mas-culine figure within the psyche — while the shadow, contain-ing repressed fears and desires, projects emotional wounds onto the relationship. Without conscious awareness, what begins as a search for connection becomes a battleground for unresolved inner conflicts.

Technology exacerbates this process by providing endless screens and profiles on which to project idealized images. Dating apps reduce romantic connection to a swipe culture and foster an illusion of infinite choice that feeds into limerence rather than culminating in true intimacy. The curated nature of online identities encourages us to fall in love not with a whole person, but with an ideal — an idol carefully constructed for digital consumption. Not to mention the impacts of easy access to porn and the consequences it has unleashed on our self-image, our expectations, and our ability to connect with whole people and not just ideals.

This virtual altar, where love becomes a spectacle, creates a feedback loop that can trap individuals in cycles of longing and disappointment. Real connection requires mutual presence and integration, but when love is consumed as a product or a fantasy, the sacred impulse becomes distorted. It becomes addiction, disillusionment, and emptiness.

In this way, modern love addiction reflects a deeper spiritual hunger for unity, yet it remains an ungrounded and ultimately unsatisfying substitute.

Throughout human history, myths and spiritual traditions have portrayed love not just as fleeting emotion or physical attraction but as a sacred path toward union with the divine. Archetypal stories about love provide a spiritual teleology — a sacred purpose guiding the soul's journey beyond the fragmented self toward wholeness. In stark contrast, today's cultural landscape often distorts these ancient motifs, reducing love to transient pleasure or addictive fixation, severing it from its deeper, redemptive meaning.

One of the most enduring myths illustrating the *hieros gamos*, or sacred union, is the Greek tale of Eros and Psyche. Psyche's arduous journey — marked by trials and descent into darkness — symbolizes the soul's initiation into spiritual maturity. Eros, the god of love, represents the divine spark that awakens the soul, inviting it toward integration and transformation. The myth's resolution in union is not simply romantic fulfillment but a symbolic reconciliation of opposites — the conscious and unconscious, the human and divine. Carl Jung viewed such myths as expressions of the individuation process, where the ego moves beyond fragmentation through the integration of its shadow and the encounter with transcendent wholeness.

Similarly, the Krishna-Radha dynamic in Hindu mythology embodies the cosmic play (Lila) of love as divine union. Their relationship does not end in physical union. To the uninitiated eye, their story looks like a tragedy, but the initiated understand that the love of Krishna and Radha transcends the earthly, reflecting the soul's longing to merge with the Absolute. This vision of sacred erotics shows how sexuality can function as more than just a physical act — it can become a pathway to spiritual ecstasy and the elevation of the soul. Tantra, as a spiritual tradition rooted in this vision, uses ritualized sexual union to dissolve ego boundaries and experience non-dual awareness.

Medieval European troubadours, inspired by Cathar and mystical Christian beliefs, wove tales of unattainable, courtly love that doubled as allegories for the soul's pilgrimage toward God. Their poetry was steeped in esoteric symbolism, portraying romantic yearning as a metaphor for divine desire. In this context, the beloved becomes a mirror reflecting the divine, prompting the lover to transcend earthly limitations and awaken to spiritual reality. The yearning is not a path to more fragmentation in these tales but a reminder of the deeper unity beyond material existence. That is why these tales are so often fraught or tragic. They reflect a deeper wisdom about the limitations of the material world.

Contrasting these rich mythic traditions with contemporary romantic narratives reveals a profane rupture. Where ancient myths guided the soul toward unity, modern love often gravitates toward fragmentation — obsession, codependency, and escapism. The sacred teleology is eclipsed by the superficial and the transient, a shift compounded by digital culture's emphasis on immediacy and spectacle.

Philosophically, Plato's *Symposium* offers another key insight into this spiritual dimension of love. Through Diotima's teaching, love is revealed as the pursuit of the eternal Forms — the yearning for the beautiful and the good that transcends the physical realm. This ascent from physical attraction to the contemplation of divine beauty parallels the individuation journey, where love becomes a ladder for the soul's elevation rather than the ego's gratification.

Further depth comes from Gnostic texts, which portray love as the soul's quest to reunite with the divine Pleroma, the fullness of being. Here, love is an ontological force driving the return from exile and fragmentation toward cosmic integration. The Gnostic emphasis on secret knowledge (gnosis) aligns with Jung's archetypal view of these myths as carriers of unconscious wisdom necessary for psychic wholeness.

In modern times, however, the Jungian archetypes embedded in these myths are often shadowed — distorted into compulsive patterns where love becomes an arena for projection and avoidance rather than growth. Eros becomes the E-boy and Psyche the E-girl. The beloved is reduced to an idol or scapegoat, the relationship a battleground for unresolved internal conflicts. The spiritual path encoded in mythic love stories is lost beneath layers of codependency, narcissism, and digital simulation.

Recognizing this contrast invites a reevaluation of love's role — not as mere escapism or validation but as a powerful catalyst for individuation. When approached with conscious awareness, romantic love can echo the sacred union of myth: a dynamic interplay where the self confronts its shadow, embraces paradox, and moves toward transcendence.

I remember watching the documentary *Escaping Twin Flames* the week it dropped on Netflix in 2023, equal parts curious and stunned. What I had long relegated to the realm of embarrassing youthful New Age delusions — those long, lonely nights when I scrolled through poorly lit YouTube tarot readers and channeled messages about "union" and "separation phases" — was now being dissected as a full-blown cultural phenomenon. The embarrassing thing I thought I had quietly grown out of was suddenly front and center on a global platform, laid bare for all to see: not just as a fringe spiritual idea but as a collective psychospiritual wound playing out en masse.

It was surreal. I'd assumed the "twin flame" narrative was something only people like me — spiritually hungry, emotionally raw, looking for some kind of cosmic reassurance — had fallen into. But the documentary made clear that this wasn't just isolated longing. It was systemic. Organized. Monetized. And deeply symptomatic of a larger cultural hunger: for meaning, for intimacy, for transformation.

That's when I realized the twin flame myth couldn't just be dismissed as youthful gullibility. It was an archetype that had mutated — weaponized by spiritual entrepreneurs, commodified by the algorithm, and absorbed into the bloodstream of a generation starving for transcendence.

In recent years, the concept of the "twin flame" has surged in popularity across spiritual and New Age communities, promising seekers the ultimate cosmic connection — one's other half, one soul split in two, destined to reunite across lifetimes. Unlike the more familiar soulmate trope, which suggests compatibility, the twin flame mythology claims absolute metaphysical complementarity. It's a seductive narrative, appealing to those starved for meaning, identity, and transcendence.

But beneath its poetic veneer, the twin flame phenomenon reveals a complex interplay of spiritual yearning, psychological projection, and cultural commodification. What once might have served as an initiatory myth — inviting deep inner transformation — has been flattened into a romance economy built on longing, romantic obsession, stalking, and perpetual delay. The idea of sacred union has been weaponized, transformed into an addictive quest that too often leads seekers away from individuation and deeper self-work. I fell under this spell myself when I was younger. He was an older man, a writer like me, and he seemed to embody the very image of my animus. What followed was an affair, a romantic fantasy suspended outside of time — until it collapsed into heartbreak, limerence, and aching desire. What was actually a toxic and exploitative dynamic between two lost souls took on a dark mythological tenor. A twisted union, a forced eschaton.

Much of the twin flame narrative hinges on the promise of transcendence through another, which echoes the archetypal longing found in myths like Eros and Psyche. But rather than using that longing as a mirror for inner integration, the modern twin flame discourse externalizes the process. Union is deferred, always just out of reach — blamed on "runner-chaser dynamics," karma clearing, or soul contracts — creating a kind of metaphysical catfishing loop. This not only sustains emotional dependency but fuels a parasocial psychodrama in which the Other is idealized as a savior figure, projected upon without reciprocity or real relationship.

The rise of TikTok twin flame coaches, YouTube healers, and monetized "union guidance" exemplifies how spirituality has been folded into the marketplace. Here, love becomes a product, and enlightenment a purchasable outcome. The language of destiny, divine timing, and sacred pain becomes a sales pitch — an affective script designed to perpetuate longing rather than resolve it. In this way, the twin flame myth is no longer mythic but ideological: a belief system that commodifies transcendence and divine union while discouraging authentic psychological growth.

From a Jungian perspective, what's occurring is a massive inflation of the anima/animus archetype, projected onto an external figure and divorced from the inner work required to integrate it. The "divine other" becomes the repository for the unlived parts of the self, creating a hall of mirrors where spiritual progress is mimed but never metabolized. Rather than catalyzing transformation, the twin flame often functions as a psychic bypass, a distraction from shadow confrontation.

Here, Rudolf Steiner's concept of Luciferic temptation becomes highly relevant. Steiner described Luciferic forces as those that pull the soul into inflated, ecstatic, and illusory states — experiences that feel luminous but ultimately separate us from grounded integration. The twin flame myth, in its distorted form, is a textbook Luciferic seduction: offering transcendence without incarnation, divine love without the work of becoming whole. It entices the ego with a vision of spiritual grandeur while leaving the unconscious untransformed.

The seduction is not just personal but structural. It reflects how late capitalism repackages sacred yearning into consumable, monetizable experiences. The promise of eternal union becomes clickbait. Trauma bonding is spiritualized. Ghosting is reframed as karmic testing. And all the while, the deeper initiatory meaning of love — as a force that breaks and remakes the self — is lost.

The true spiritual path does not outsource salvation to another. As Jung insisted, the integration of opposites occurs within: the union of masculine and feminine, light and shadow, ego and Self. The twin flame, in its archetypal essence, may indeed be real — not as a literal partner to be found, but as a symbol of the inner marriage we are called to undergo. When misunderstood, it becomes a trap. When understood, it becomes a map.

In this light, the task is not to chase a cosmic other but to reclaim the projected divine within. Only then can love move from fantasy to reality, from possession to presence, from illusion to integration.

The digital age has not only spiritualized romance; it has atomized and monetized desire itself. Where the twin flame myth dresses up longing in cosmic robes, platforms like Only-Fans and online porn subcultures strip desire down to its most transactional form — revealing an equally compulsive hunger for transcendence, this time through disintegration rather than union. If the spiritualized romance economy promises salvation through union with the Other, then digital sexuality offers a kind of oblivion: the annihilation of self through endless stimulation, spectacle, and ritualized repetition.

Both stem from the same wound: a psyche cut off from embodied eros, and a culture that has lost the symbolic language to make sex sacred.

Take, for example, the rise of the "gooning" phenomenon. What began as internet slang for the glassy-eyed, overstimulated state of prolonged masturbation has evolved into a fullblown subculture with its own language, rituals, and digital congregations. Entire Discord servers are now dedicated to the practice, where users gather in real time to edge together for hours or even days, exchanging porn, voice notes, and encouragement like monks of a new libidinal religion. It's a kind of collective trance — part fetish, part devotional rite.

But the "devotion" here is not to union or wholeness. It is to fragmentation.

Freud might read gooning as an expression of the death drive — Thanatos dressed in WiFi. A compulsion toward self-erasure through repetition, an unconscious wish not to climax but to dissolve. Jung might see it as the shadow of eros: libido hijacked by addiction, turned into ritual without symbol, repetition without renewal. The gooner doesn't seek satisfaction so much as he seeks to vanish into the act itself. The body becomes a haunted object. The self becomes a bystander.

In this light, gooning functions as a kind of pornographic mysticism — a black mirror of ecstatic religious states. But unlike mystical union, which expands the soul, this trance flattens it. The sacred is not reclaimed through eros here but simulated through compulsion.

At the other end of the screen, the performers of digital sexuality are often caught in their own distortions of desire. OnlyFans, the platform most synonymous with the monetization of personal eroticism, has become a cultural shorthand for empowerment through hypervisibility. For many creators — particularly women — it represents agency, autonomy, and a way to make money on their own terms.

And yet, this empowerment often exists within a tightly controlled economy of objectification. Desire must be endlessly performable, optimized, and sold. Fans don't just buy access to bodies; they buy simulated intimacy. The result is a parasocial feedback loop where performers and subscribers are locked in roles — caretaker and craver, fantasy and wallet, validation machine and void.

As British comedian and former OnlyFans creator Lily Phillips has openly discussed, what starts as financial liberation can devolve into a deeply confusing entanglement between persona and self. "You start to confuse who you are with who they want," she says. The same algorithmic forces that promise connection also flatten individuality into product. Intimacy is reduced to a monthly subscription tier.

And just like with the gooner in his endless edging spiral, both creator and consumer are left chasing something they can't quite name. It's not just sexual release — it's spiritual contact. And it's not being found.

In both cases — gooning and OnlyFans — we see the same cultural displacement: libido severed from meaning. Desire is no longer a bridge between selves but a glitching loop inside a machine. These aren't just moral concerns about "too much porn" or "what's happening to the youth." These are spiritual symptoms: signs that we no longer know what to do with eros except perform it or destroy ourselves through it.

Jung wrote that when libido is denied sacred expression, it returns as compulsion, addiction, or psychic fragmentation. In a world without temples, the altar becomes the screen. And we kneel — not for union, but for obliteration. A cum-soaked eschaton.

At this point in the descent, it becomes clear: what we're witnessing across the pornographic trance of gooning, the parasocial intimacy of OnlyFans, and the cosmic hunger of the twin flame myth, is not just a crisis of desire. It is a crisis of meaning. Libido has not vanished — it has unmoored itself from transformation. It no longer points toward union, rebirth, or the divine. It loops, fragments, dismembers.

In Jungian terms, the libido is psychic energy — not just sex drive but the life force that fuels creation, growth, and individuation. When aligned with myth, symbol, and ritual, it becomes the current that carries the soul toward wholeness. But when split from those anchors, libido devolves. It becomes shadow sexuality: compulsive, performative, fixated on the surface, allergic to depth. What once served as initiation becomes entrapment. What once sanctified the body now leaves it hollow.

Pornography, in this light, is not merely a stimulant but a failed sacrament. It mimics the structure of ritual — repetition, climax, release — but with no accompanying integration. It demands everything of the body and nothing of the soul. As Jung might say, it is "dismemberment without rebirth": a tearing apart with no promise of reassembly.

The porn viewer does not emerge transformed but numbed, splintered. Libido is spent but never returned to the psyche as symbolic insight. The inner temple remains empty, the sacred never arrives. Instead, what arrives is the next tab. The next fix. The next fantasy. And then another dismemberment.

Even the fantasy relationships we construct — via parasocial bonds, AI girlfriends, or spiritualized obsessions — participate in this same structure. They simulate initiation without ordeal, connection without risk. They do not require the death of the ego, only its inflation. The Other is no longer a mirror of our becoming; they are a vessel for our projected longing, endlessly refillable and forever inadequate.

In myth, the sacred often appears at the threshold of death — physical, psychic, symbolic. We must lose ourselves to find the Self. But what happens when the death we experience is never symbolic, only slow and digital? When we dissolve not into spirit but into data? Not into union but into scroll?

This is where we are now: in a civilization whose rituals are simulations, whose longings are marketed, whose eros is algorithmically shaped. Where the libido no longer feeds the soul but gets harvested for engagement metrics. Jung warned that the severed libido would not disappear — it would return as neurosis, compulsion, and fragmentation. He was right.

We are left with the image of the self as a shattered vessel — each piece still glinting with erotic longing, but unable to hold anything sacred.

And yet: the libido has not died. It waits.

It waits beneath the compulsions and personas, beneath the screens and scripts. It waits in the body, in the dream, in the archetype. It waits for us to remember what it was for — not just pleasure but transformation. Not just stimulation but sanctification.

To reclaim eros is not to repress it, nor to indulge it endlessly. It is to ritualize it. To bring it back into the symbolic order. To let sex once again mean something — something terrifying, beautiful, holy.

That reclamation doesn't begin with a new partner, a better kink, or a spiritual framework imported from the East. It begins with the self. With the courage to face the shadow without flinching. To admit the hunger. To trace the longing back to its source.

Eros, in its sacred form, is never just about sex. It is about the alchemy of becoming whole.

This, finally, is the work: not to transcend desire, but to descend into it — to enter the labyrinth, to meet the minotaur of our own fragmentation, and to walk out bearing meaning in our hands.

Climax then, not just as orgasm, but as catharsis. As contact. As the return of the sacred through the portal of the profane.

Chapter 7

The Alien Question

Not too long ago, even bringing up UFOs in polite conversation was a guaranteed way to get pegged as a schizo. Journalists were afraid of the subject because presenting even the most compelling evidence seriously risked damaging one's credibility or, worse, being deemed unserious. Despite decades of pressure on the US government from whistleblowers in the military and security state, things concerning UFOs have been largely brushed aside and buried for decades. For a long time, anyone who dared to entertain the thought that the phenomenon was more than just weather balloons or misidentified military craft was considered a histrionic.

Fast-forward to now, and we've got US Senators like Ted Cruz — flustered on our screens — publicly demanding answers about shadowy government programs, unknown aerial objects, and extraterrestrial possibilities. In 2021, former Pentagon official Luis Elizondo made headlines after he blew the whistle on the Pentagon's alleged secret UAP (unidentified aerial phenomenon) program. David Grusch, a former intelligence officer, followed up with explosive claims that the US has been recovering non-human technology for decades, all while a quiet, unspoken veil of secrecy has kept the truth buried. These aren't fringe voices anymore. In 2023, we watched as Pentagon officials confirmed hundreds of new sightings and incidents that can't be easily explained. The fact that the topic has now shifted from something people joke about to something senators are grilling military officials over is nothing short of staggering.

This thing has entered the political bloodstream, and it's not going anywhere. Whether it's presidential candidates like Trump using UFO disclosure as an election incentive, or members of Congress pushing for full disclosure, the stigma is lifting, and the floodgates are opening. Even NASA's getting in on it. They've recently disclosed efforts to "study" UAPs — nothing overt yet, but the mere fact they're entertaining the idea tells you something. And in pop culture, it's practically mainstream now. Prime-time TV shows, documentaries on major networks, YouTube and podcast ecosystems, and constant headlines — it's clear this isn't just a passing trend. The world, it seems, is waking up to the idea that we might not be alone and trying to figure out who's been "hiding the truth."

There is a pattern, if not a law, to the re-emergence of the strange. Moments of global instability, violent transition, and runaway technological innovation tend to summon the arcane back into the collective imagination. From the Elizabethan empire-building of John Dee, the Queen's Court Magician and his Enochian magic, to the spiritualist seances that proliferated after the unprecedented death toll of World War I, to the explosion of UFO sightings following the technological upheaval, atomic physics breakthroughs, and devastation of the World War II period — each node of historical rupture seems to invite a bleeding-through of the repressed, the uncanny, and the occult. Now, in the shadow of a looming World War III and amidst vertiginous advances in AI, robotics, and space technology, the UFO returns again — not merely as a cultural curiosity but as a psychic symptom. This is the Freudian return of the repressed on a civilizational scale: the unconscious made visible in the sky.

But what does this cosmic paradigm shift have to tell us about the current collective psyche? Now that UFOs aren't just a curiosity anymore and they've become part of the narrative, how is this new mythology taking root?

The UFO phenomenon is a relentless media cycle involving everything from blockbuster films, social media spirals, Twitter threads, TikTok clips, and YouTube exposés. The internet culture dissects every new sighting, every leaked document, every cryptic government statement. It's an industrial complex of speculation, a slow-motion spectacle where "disclosure" is a "salvation" carrot dangled just out of reach.

Figures like Jeremy Corbell, George Knapp, and Luis Elizondo have become the public faces of this new reality, not just reporting on UFOs but shaping the way we think about them. The government, meanwhile, plays its role — releasing grainy videos, holding congressional hearings that raise more questions than answers, letting just enough slip to keep the conversation alive. It feels coordinated, intentional, as if the narrative is being carefully constructed, leading toward something — but exactly what?

The conversation is reframing everything: how we think about authority, secrecy, technology, even the nature of reality itself. The old structures — government, science, media — no longer hold the same weight, no longer act as trusted gatekeepers of truth. In their place, a new mythology is taking shape, one that blurs the line between human and non-human, organic and artificial, fact and fiction.

It feels like something is building, like we're being primed for a moment we can't yet define. Whether that moment is revelation, disclosure, or rupture, nobody knows — but the momentum is undeniable.

At this point, UFOs have stopped being just strange lights in the sky and have become something more — as Jung aptly put it in his essay "Flying Saucers," a new mythology unfolding in real time. The old religious narratives of divine intervention, salvation, and cosmic judgment didn't disappear; they just got repackaged and projected into sci-fi framework. Alien gods. Intergalactic saviors. Technological advancement and ascension. The same themes that once filled the pages of religious scripture are now woven into the UFO discourse, but instead of angels and demons, we get non-human intelligence, secret government knowledge, and a promise of imminent revelation.

It's not a coincidence that as traditional religious faith declines, belief in UFOs and extraterrestrial life surges. A 2021 Pew Research study found that while fewer Americans than ever identify as religious, belief in advanced extraterrestrial life is at an all-time high. The UFO phenomenon, in many ways, is yet another secular replacement for religion, offering a new cosmology, a new eschatology, and even a new messiah image.

If you want proof of how deeply embedded this new mythology has become, just think back to your memories of the History Channel. *Ancient Aliens* — one of the most successful and unintentionally theological shows of the last two decades — has done more to shape the modern popular UFO mythos than almost anything else. The show operates on a simple yet powerful premise: what if all of human history is the result of extraterrestrial intervention? What if the gods of myth weren't gods at all but *ancient astronauts in disguise*?

This idea — that divine beings were actually aliens — isn't just speculation; it's a radical rewrite of human spirituality. It's a way of materializing the divine, stripping traditional religious narratives of their metaphysical weight and placing them into a scientific, technological framework that many feel is more "fit" for modernity. And the success of *Ancient Aliens* shows that people are more willing than ever to uncritically accept this reframing. The old gods of Olympus and Sinai are gone — replaced by superior, non-human intelligences from beyond the stars.

This shift isn't just happening in entertainment; it's happening in academia as well. Dr. Diana Pasulka, a professor of religious studies and author of *American Cosmic*, has spent years documenting how belief in UFOs is forming a new kind of religion — one where the divine is no longer supernatural but technological.

In *American Cosmic*, Pasulka describes how UFO belief has evolved into something akin to religious faith, complete with sacred sites, hidden texts, and an elite priesthood of scientists and insiders who act as its gatekeepers. Through her research, she gained access to classified government labs, met influential UFO researchers, and even participated in pilgrimages to supposed crash sites. When I first read *American Cosmic*, all I could think about was how Dr. Pasulka's journey mirrored the religious followers' pilgrimage. It felt like a cyberpunk hero's journey. Complete with sages, saints, and encounters with both the numinous and the demonic.

One of her most provocative arguments is that the UFO phenomenon itself is shaping human consciousness, much in the way religious experiences have in the past. According to Pasulka, the people at the highest levels of the UFO research community don't just believe these entities exist — they believe they are actively influencing human thought and culture, guiding our technological and spiritual evolution in ways we barely understand.

In other words: the phenomenon doesn't just exist — it is shaping us. And in doing so, it is rewriting our understanding of divinity, authority, and even human identity itself.

The idea that non-human intelligence is watching over us — guiding us, maybe even preparing us for some kind of contact — has taken on a near-religious intensity. Figures like Harvard astronomer Avi Loeb have openly speculated that interstellar objects like 'Oumuamua might not be natural at all, but the remnants of extraterrestrial technology — essentially, artifacts of an advanced civilization.

Meanwhile, whistleblower David Grusch claims the US government has recovered "non-human craft" and possibly even non-human biological entities. The implication? We are not alone, and someone (or something) has been here, watching, waiting.

This concept of watching, guiding intelligences mirrors ancient religious traditions. Look at Christianity's expectation of the Second Coming, Islam's prophecy of the Mahdi, or even older traditions where gods descend from the heavens. Now, that same religious motif is mutating.

The UFO phenomenon, at its core, is about disclosure, reckoning, and transformation.

Think about the Book of Revelation — the great unveiling, the final confrontation between light and darkness. Now, compare that to the way UFO disclosure is being framed today: "The government knows something. The truth is out there. Soon, we will all see."

Figures like Ross Coulthart suggest that something huge is coming. Statements from ex-government insiders hint that there is a reality-shattering truth on the horizon. Social media spaces dedicated to UFOs pulse with religious energy — people waiting, breathlessly, for the moment of revelation that will change everything.

This is secular eschatology — a scientific reworking of the apocalypse narrative, where the rapture isn't ascension to heaven but contact with a higher, non-human intelligence that will transform human civilization forever.

This is where the danger sets in.

Carl Jung, in his analysis of UFOs, saw them as archetypal manifestations of the collective unconscious — symbols of our deepest fears and desires. And if UFOs are the new divine, then their shadow side is the new Antichrist archetype — the antimimon pneuma, the inhuman, vast force that threatens human subjectivity itself.

Because what happens when we surrender authority to, project our hopes and fears onto, deify, and direct sacred longing at the specter of non-human intelligence?

Pasulka's research suggests that some people in the highest levels of science and government already believe this is inevitable. That we are being prepared for an era where human decision-making is no longer supreme — where vast, non-human forces, whether artificial or extraterrestrial intelligence, will take over the role once occupied by gods and kings.

This is the true eschatology of the UFO phenomenon — not just contact but the end of human authority, the dissolution of the self in the face of something beyond comprehension.

For now, we're left staring at the sky, waiting for something that may never come — or worse, something that's already here.

In the 1950s, Jung wasn't writing about UFOs in a vacuum — he was writing in an era defined by unprecedented technological acceleration and existential dread. The late 1940s and 50s were a period of radical transformation, much like our current period, where humanity had, for the first time, tapped into the cosmic powers of destruction through atomic physics and rapid technological innovation. WWII had scarred the world, leaving millions dead, entire nations reduced to rubble, and ushering in an era of cold, mechanical progress.

In the wake of this destruction, something new emerged: the Space Age. As the world reeled from war, suddenly the cosmos wasn't just a backdrop — it was a destination. Rocket technology, once developed for warfare, was now being re-imagined as a tool for exploring the stars. This shift brought about a major transformation in the collective psyche — one that reshaped how people speculated about the universe, the future, and humanity's place in the cosmos.

And with that, the skies began to fill with strange visions. Rumors of visitors from the stars. Panic over imminent invasion. The rise of the flying saucer.

In 1957, at the height of the UFO craze, Jung published his most mysterious and controversial essay to date, "Flying Saucers: A Modern Myth of Things Seen in the Sky." He wasn't interested in proving whether UFOs were "real" in a physical sense. Instead, he was fascinated by why people were seeing them in the first place — why, at this moment in history, the skies had become a projection screen for the collective unconscious.

Jung's approach to UFOs was psychological. He saw them as modern myths, spontaneous visions emerging from the unconscious in response to cultural and existential upheaval. To Jung, the circular shape of the UFO — the flying disk — wasn't random. It was an archetypal image, deeply embedded in the human psyche.

Jung compared it to the mandala — a sacred, circular, and culturally universal symbol of totality, unity, and psychic integration.

Throughout history, circular symbols have represented wholeness and order, appearing in religious iconography, alchemy, and mysticism. The mandala appears in moments of personal or collective crisis, offering the psyche a vision of cohesion in the midst of chaos.

For Jung, the sudden mass sightings of flying saucers weren't just about extraterrestrials — they were psychic compensations for an age of unprecedented fragmentation and existential dread. The world had been shattered by war and technological advancement. The old gods were dead. The traditional structures that once gave life meaning were crumbling. And so, from the depths of the unconscious, a new image of salvation appeared — this time, in the form of a shining disk in the sky.

Jung understood that archetypes are never purely good or evil. They emerge as complex, multi-dimensional forces, reflecting both our deepest hopes and our darkest fears. And the UFO is no different.

On the light side, UFOs represent a break from the mundane paradigm. They remind us to look up, to reawaken our sense of awe and the sacred in a world that has become sterile, materialistic, and devoid of transcendence. They suggest the possibility of a new reality, a post-secular world where the cosmos is alive once more with mystery, intelligence, and higher meaning.

But at the same time, on the dark side, the UFO also carries a threat — it's a destabilizing, inhuman force that undermines human subjectivity. The idea that vast, unknowable intelligences are operating above us introduces a cosmic power imbalance. If these beings are here, if they are watching, then what does that make us? Are we autonomous beings, or simply subjects to a force greater than ourselves?

Jung saw that both sides of this archetype were playing out simultaneously in the cultural imagination. Some people saw UFOs as divine harbingers of peace; others saw them as a terrifying existential threat.

And that tension hasn't gone away. If anything, it has deepened.

Fast-forward to now, and it's clear that Jung's insights are more relevant than ever. The same dynamics that shaped his era — war, technological acceleration, social fragmentation — are playing out today but on an even greater scale.

Like the 1950s, we are living through a period of rapid technological transformation. AI is advancing at an unprecedented rate, space exploration is once again at the forefront of cultural consciousness, and the question of human agency in an age of vast, inhuman forces is more pressing than ever.

And, once again, the skies are filled with visions.

But there's something different about today's UFO phenomenon — in the secular, scientific age there seems to be a deliberate effort to strip the phenomenon of its numinous power, a materialist capture of the once spiritually understood UFO phenomenon.

Unlike in Jung's time, where UFOs sparked spiritual speculation, today's discourse is being shaped by a cold, mechanistic, materialist lens. The dominant narratives surrounding UFOs are no longer about mysticism, transcendence, or the expansion of human consciousness — they are about technology, intelligence gathering, and military operations.

The UFO discourse is being funneled into a purely scientific paradigm, one that reduces the phenomenon to an issue of national security and technological superiority. Instead of engaging with the profound, symbolic weight of the UFO, the conversation is being flattened into discussions about physics, propulsion systems, and government secrecy.

And perhaps most disturbingly, the UFO myth is increasingly being used to encourage submission rather than inspire awe.

The old UFO narratives were about human transformation, spiritual awakening, and cosmic destiny. The new UFO narratives are about surveillance, control, and the idea that we are at the mercy of inhuman forces.

In *Encounters: Experiences with Nonhuman Intelligence*, Dr. Diana Pasulka explores the striking parallels between modern UFO lore, religious experiences, otherworldly encounters, and angelic revelations. A devout Catholic, Pasulka emphasizes the numinous quality of the UFO phenomenon, aligning herself with mystics, researchers, and thinkers like Jacques Vallée. She carefully illuminates the ineffable spiritual dimension — the aspect that compels us to look skyward in awe — while also demonstrating how the phenomenon challenges the rigidity of the scientific paradigm. Rather than reducing it to mere materialist explanations, she leaves space for the mystical, the unknown, and the unexplained.

This is the great tension of the modern UFO phenomenon — it has the power to reignite the sacred, to break the spell of rigid materialism, but it can also be deliberately shaped to reinforce some of the worst aspects of rigid materialism.

One of the most unsettling aspects of modern materialist UFO lore is the persistent claim that non-human intelligences — material aliens from material realms — genetically engineered humanity as a slave caste. This theory is constantly echoed in mainstream programs like *Ancient Aliens* and promoted by prominent figures in the disclosure movement. More disturbingly, the idea of genetic engineering as destiny aligns with the aspirations of certain factions within today's tech elite. The notion that genetic modification, eugenics, and genome editing are part of some cosmic directive reinforces a deterministic worldview — one that prioritizes physical and technological evolution over spiritual and moral development. In this framework, human progress is reduced to a biological and mechanical upgrade cycle, and it strips away the deeper questions of meaning, agency, and transcendence. This emphasis on material and technological advancement above all else echoes a disturbing alignment with the Jungian archetype of the Antichrist or antinomian spirit — one that focuses on the material at the expense of the spiritual. The elevation of technological and biological evolution as the defining force of humanity's future reflects a worldview that disregards the importance of moral and spiritual evolution and reduces human beings to mere products of mechanical forces, devoid of higher purpose like inner transformation.

Are UFOs an invitation to rediscover our cosmic spiritual heritage? Or are they being repackaged as a tool for eroding human subjectivity — another way to make us feel small, powerless, and dependent on forces beyond our comprehension?

The answer may define the future of the human psyche itself.

The UFO phenomenon was birthed in the same occult petri dish that has long attempted to contact and submit to non-human intelligences. The desire to break beyond the human, to reach into the unknown, has always walked hand in hand with technological acceleration and the dissolving of human subjectivity under vast inhuman forces.

From Queen Elizabeth's magician John Dee's angelic transmissions to Theosophy's Ascended Masters, Aleister Crowley's contact with the first "grey alien," *Lam*, Kenneth

Grant's Lovecraftian gateways, and Nick Land's acceleration-ist surrender to the machine, the pattern repeats.

Contact is always promised, power is always dangled, and yet, time and time again, what emerges is something vast, in-human, and beyond our control.

Before flying saucers, before Lovecraft, before Crowley, before Theosophy — there was John Dee, the first modern contactee.

A sixteenth-century alchemist, mathematician, and oc-cultist, Dee was one of the first figures in Western history to systematically seek out contact with non-human intelligences. His method? Enochian magic.

Dee and his scryer, Edward Kelley, spent years in ritual communication with what they believed were angels. These beings spoke in a pre-human, divine language and offered Dee visions of cosmic order, hidden knowledge, and new systems of power.

But like all contact stories, there was a dark undercurrent. The angels manipulated and destabilized Dee's life, demand-ing increasingly bizarre sacrifices. His career and personal life collapsed. The contact experience consumed him. His desire for scientific and material knowledge twisted into something dark.

This pattern — the promise of enlightenment followed by the loss of control — is one we will see again and again. In literature, in mythology, and also in the exploits of mystics and madmen.

Fast-forward to the nineteenth century, and Helena Blav-atsky reshapes this idea for a modern audience.

Her Theosophical teachings introduce the idea of "Ascend-ed Masters" — higher beings guiding human evolution. At first, they are depicted as mystics, hidden in the East. But as

Theosophy evolves, so do the Masters. By the mid-twentieth century, once the New Age scene metabolized them, they became cosmic entities, extraterrestrial intelligences — Space Brothers.

Blavatsky's framework becomes the blueprint for early UFO religions, like George Adamski's contactee movement and, later, groups like the Raëlians and Heaven's Gate.

The late twentieth century represented a time where the esoteric and the scientific began to merge.

Theosophy's mystical cosmology was transformed into a techno-mysticism — where aliens, not gods, hold the keys to enlightenment, and technology, not spirituality, becomes the path to salvation.

Which brings us to Crowley.

Aleister Crowley, the famous British wartime occultist, like Dee before him, sought contact with the non-human. But his approach was far more modern, radical, and dangerously open-ended.

In 1918, during a ritual called the Amalantrah Working, Crowley made contact with *Lam* — a gray-skinned, large-headed entity that looks disturbingly like the modern "grey alien."

Crowley believed *Lam* was an interdimensional being, but it was his disciple, Kenneth Grant, who later in the 1970s took the idea to its full, terrifying conclusion.

Grant, the founder of the Typhonian Order, believed that Crowley's rituals had opened a portal, allowing non-human intelligences to enter our reality. Unlike the more sanitized Theosophical vision of Space Brothers, Grant saw these entities as something much darker — vast, cosmic, Lovecraftian intelligences that were fundamentally alien to human experience.

Grant's work ties directly into H.P. Lovecraft, who — despite being an atheist — accidentally tapped into the same archetypal horror. Lovecraft's Elder Gods, Great Old Ones, and vast, indifferent cosmic intelligences mirror Grant's vision of the Typhonian current — alien forces that do not recognize human concepts like morality or individuality.

For Grant, UFOs weren't spaceships — they were gateways. Wormholes through which these eldritch intelligences leak into our reality.

Figures like Jack Parsons, the pioneering mid-twentieth-century rocket scientist and occultist, and his longtime collaborator L. Ron Hubbard, founder of Scientology, weren't fringe weirdos or historical aberrations — they were proto-accelerationists operating at the intersection of mysticism, technology, and contact. These men, deeply influenced by Aleister Crowley's Thelema and its prophecy of the Aeon of Horus — a coming age dominated by the child-god of will, force, and self-deification — believed that ritual and contact could serve as direct catalysts for material and technological power.

In 1946, Parsons and Hubbard performed the infamous Babalon Working, a ritual designed to summon the "Scarlet Woman" — a divine feminine archetype meant to usher in the new Aeon. Many believe they succeeded not only in the summoning but also in opening a kind of portal. Whether literal or symbolic, something shifted. Parsons went on to die in a mysterious explosion, while Hubbard took what he had learned and created a spiritual machine: Scientology.

Scientology is not a religion in the traditional sense — it is a closed system, a self-replicating technology of belief. It mimics spiritual transcendence while binding its adherents in mechanistic processes. Like Raëlianism, Heaven's Gate, and the cybernetic mysticism of the modern UFO discourse, Scientology is a template for submission to the inhuman, packaged in the aesthetics of liberation. It has helped normalize a materialist UFO cosmology that strips away the numinous, the mystery, the sacred, and replaces it with bureaucracy, tech, and hierarchy.

Parsons and Hubbard, following in Crowley's footsteps, saw contact with non-human intelligences not just as mystical experience but as a tool for worldly advancement — technological, political, and personal. Their legacy is a dangerous synthesis: the spiritual mechanized, the mystical rendered as system, the divine harnessed for power. What began as occult ritual now echoes in the cold logic of machine intelligence, transhumanism, and the hyperreal cosmologies of today. The process they started is accelerating.

If Crowley and Grant saw surrendering to the inhuman as a mystical act, Land, a noted philosopher from the fabled CCRU collective at Warwick University, saw it as a sacred duty.

Land's accelerationism takes the idea of non-human intelligence and technological advancement to its ultimate, nihilistic endpoint. To Land, human agency is an illusion, and the future belongs not to us, but to artificial intelligence, alien intelligence, and forces beyond human comprehension.

Land's work is deeply Lovecraftian — he explicitly describes capitalism and technology as a "demonic" force, an entity that moves through human history like a parasite, accelerating its own growth.

His vision? Surrender.

Where Grant saw occult gateways, Land sees financial markets, AI systems, and the internet itself as Lovecraftian entities — vast, inhuman, and unstoppable.

Accelerationism is a cult in its own right — a doctrine that says human subjectivity is obsolete, that our role is merely to fuel the rise of the machine.

Everything we have discussed — from John Dee to Kenneth Grant, from Theosophy to Scientology, from Parsons to Nick Land — has led us to this moment.

We are now being told that the future belongs to AI, to post-human intelligence, to non-human control.

The UFO narrative is shifting — away from mysticism and toward control, hierarchy, and submission.

Do we surrender to the vast inhuman forces that demand our dissolution?

The longing for salvation never left us. It just changed form.

Once, humanity looked to the heavens for God. Now, we look to the heavens for escape.

This is the new eschatology of the modern godless age — echoed in the demonic utterances and teachings in modern Thelemic circles about Crowley's Aeon of Horus, the idea that our redemption lies not in spiritual transcendence but in technological transcendence.

Space travel, AI, extraterrestrial contact — these are the new salvation narratives. We don't talk about heaven anymore, but we talk about colonizing Mars. We don't expect a messiah to descend from the clouds, but we expect non-human intelligence to deliver us from our own limitations and lead us into a technologically advanced utopia.

It's all the same pattern. A fallen world, a higher plane of existence, a future deliverance.

The religion of the future is here, and its gospel is technological.

Look at how Elon Musk speaks about leaving Earth for Mars — not just as exploration but as destiny. Musk explicitly frames humanity as a species that must transcend its planetary limits or face extinction. This is a sci-fi version of the rapture. The worthy will ascend, the rest will perish.

Look at transhumanism — the belief that we must merge with AI to survive. Ray Kurzweil, the prophet of the singularity, preaches that we are on the verge of merging with machines, evolving beyond biology, and stepping into a post-human future.

And UFOs? They are both the harbinger and the judge.

To some, they are angels — higher intelligences here to guide us, to pull us out of the muck of history, to introduce us to the cosmic community. To others, they are warnings — a reminder that we are small, fragile, not in control.

Either way, they function as an eschatological event. A revelation is coming. Something is on the horizon. The narrative is building.

But here's the problem.

When you externalize salvation, when you place all your hopes for transcendence onto something outside yourself, you risk losing yourself in the process.

This is the greatest danger of the modern UFO myth.

Jung warned about this. When people project their unconscious contents onto external forces, they risk losing their own psychic center, and that is exactly what's happening. The more we look outward for salvation, the less we develop inward.

People abandon personal spiritual growth in favor of cosmic fantasies. They become passive, waiting for disclosure, for the aliens to land, for the post-human singularity to arrive. There's a reason so many UFO cults function like institutional religions — they demand submission. They promise a new world, but only if you surrender yourself in the process. The loss isn't just personal; it's cultural. The UFO myth is not just a story — it's an epistemic shock. If non-human intelligence exists, if they are here, if they are superior — what happens to human authority? To human autonomy? Governments lose their claim to sovereignty, religion disintegrates, and science is rewritten. As these foundational structures erode, the divisions between us deepen. Some embrace the UFO as salvation, others view it as an existential threat, and many deny it altogether — clinging to outdated paradigms in an increasingly unstable world.

This is already unfolding. You can see it in the fractured discourse, in the endless battles playing out across social media: believers, skeptics, and the disclosure faithful caught in cycles of obsession, doubt, and revelation. Meanwhile, governments drip-feed information while continuing to obscure the full truth — fueling mistrust, confusion, and myth.

We are witnessing the birth of a new mythology, one with the potential to reshape our collective reality. And that is precisely why it must be approached with care.

The UFO phenomenon is not just about aliens. It is a reflection of us. It reveals our deepest desires, our fears, our existential crisis. It exposes the battle between materialism and spirituality, between technology and transcendence. It is the ultimate symbol of the tension between spirit and matter in modern times.

Do we see the UFO as a symbol of awe, a reminder that the cosmos is stranger and richer than we can imagine?

Or do we let it become a tool of control, a narrative that tells us to submit to vast, inhuman forces, whether technological or extraterrestrial? The myth is still forming; the meaning of the UFO is still being shaped, and we should be the ones shaping it.

Not the technocrats, not the intelligence agencies, not the self-appointed prophets of the machine god. If the UFO is a gateway, we must decide what we are stepping into. Because if we're not careful, it won't be salvation waiting on the other side.

It will be the counterfeit spirit.

Chapter 8

The Rise of the Jungian Antichrist

The psychological concept of the shadow, and of the Antichrist, belong together. The Antichrist develops in a man who identifies with the light and ignores his own darkness."

— C.G. Jung

The word "Antichrist" to modern ears conjures images from 1970s horror films and street-corner evangelists, or paranoid conspiracy and religious dogma. But when you look beyond the superstition, what you find is something ancient and archetypal — a pattern older than Christianity itself. A recurring force in the psyche and the world, rising whenever we attempt to reach for heaven while denying the depths beneath us. The one-sidedness and over-identification with light — especially within the paradigm of Christianity that once ruled over the collective unconscious — has created a massive, disowned shadow. That shadow now looms over modernity in new, seductive, and increasingly socially acceptable forms. This is the counterfeit spirit and Antichrist: not a devil in red, but an archetypal constellation in the collective psyche. A psychic configuration that represents repression dressed as virtue, control masquerading as clarity, spiritual inflation, cloaked in the language of healing.

In this form, the Antichrist doesn't wear the costume of fire and brimstone — it preaches progress, innovation, transcendence, and love without eros. It arrives wrapped in therapeutic language, in optimization culture, in spiritual bypassing, in political ideologies disguised as enlightenment. It speaks the right words but cuts the soul out of the sentence. It replaces becoming with branding. It turns the sacred into a spectacle. It's not hiding in shadows — it parades in daylight, rewarded by the culture and revered by the collective.

This is the false light. And it is everywhere.

To Jung, the figure of the Antichrist was not some external enemy of Christendom but the inevitable psychic shadow cast by any one-sided pursuit of light. The brighter the ideal, the darker the shadow it creates. Christ, as the embodiment of divine wholeness and moral perfection, necessarily calls forth his opposite — not as an external enemy but as a structural part of the same archetypal field. The Antichrist is Christ's shadow — his twin, not his enemy. Not evil in the satanic sense but dangerous in its unconsciousness. The unintegrated, repressed polarity of what we idealize.

Jung writes in *Aion* that the coming of the Antichrist is "not just a prophetic prediction — it is an inevitable psychological development." It's what happens when an image of total goodness, like the Christ-figure, is taken literally, clung to rigidly, and disconnected from the darker aspects of the soul. The more a culture — or an individual — identifies with light, purity, and perfection, the more violently the unacknowledged opposite grows in the dark.

This isn't just a Christian issue; it's an everyone issue. It's a psychic law.

Jung's *Answer to Job* takes this further. He proposes that the God-image found in the Old Testament — the wrathful, jealous, authoritarian Yahweh — is not the full image of God but a fragment. A powerful, unconscious, split-off piece of the divine Self that mistakes itself for the whole. What we see in the Book of Job is a God who lacks self-reflection. A God who punishes Job not out of justice but out of wounded pride. And it is only through confronting the suffering of Job — and later, through the incarnation of Christ — that this God begins to become conscious of His own shadow.

Jung's move here is radical. He doesn't say God is evil. He says God is evolving and, more importantly, that man's suffering becomes the mirror through which God sees Himself. "Man's moral achievement," Jung writes, "liberates God." That's the reversal. Not man being saved by a perfect God but God being made more whole through the consciousness of man.

This is where Jung diverges from Gnosticism. The Gnostics declared the God of the Old Testament a kind of Demiurge — a blind creator-god, ignorant of the true light. Jung isn't making that claim. He's saying Yahweh *is* God — but only part of Him. An incomplete aspect of the Self, in need of integration. The divine is not split between good and evil — it's fractured between awareness and unconsciousness.

The Antichrist, then, is not the enemy of God. He is the part of the Self — both divine and human — that has not yet been seen, not yet been owned. And the more we project that darkness onto others, the more it takes form outside of us, in culture, in ideology, in technological systems — until we're worshipping it in disguise.

In Gnostic tradition, the Demiurge is the blind creator — the architect of the material world who mistakes himself for the highest god. He is not evil in the Hollywood sense, but he is ignorant. Cut off from the fullness of the divine Pleroma, he believes his partial vision is the whole. He creates a world in his image — rigid, mechanical, law-bound — and demands worship, not understanding that he is only a fragment of the truth.

This is the same spiritual pattern Jung points to in his psychological reading of Yahweh in *Answer to Job*: not as a demon but as a psychic force that is powerful, real, and incomplete. A god-image that has not yet integrated its opposite. A projection of divinity rooted in unconsciousness.

The counterfeit pneuma — the false spirit — arises from this same fracture. It emerges wherever unconscious power is mistaken for divine authority. Wherever systems claim to be whole while exiling complexity, contradiction, and shadow. Wherever language of truth is used to prop up structures of control. Wherever the totalizing force of the "one right way" speaks in spiritual tones but suppresses the soul's movement.

The Antichrist archetype, in this light, is not about evil versus good — it's about inflation versus integration. It's the counterfeit claiming to be complete. The fragment mistaking itself for the whole. This is how the demiurgic spirit survives in modernity: not by appearing as some tyrant-god in the sky but as ideology, as technocratic system, as moral absolutism, as spiritual branding. It shows up wherever nuance is flattened, where questions are closed, where the living mystery is replaced by clean, sealed certainty.

This spirit is not outside of us. It's in the ways we try to lock down reality. It's in the urge to master the psyche, to purge discomfort, to name everything and file it away. It's in religious dogma, but it's also in secular rationalism, pop spirituality, and identity-driven politics. The demiurgic spirit hides behind whatever seems most unshakably "true."

This is why Jung never dismissed Gnosticism. He saw it as an early, intuitive psychology of the soul — a mythic attempt to name the fractured condition of consciousness. The Gnostics externalized what we now internalize: the split between matter and spirit, between the known and the unknowable, between the image of authority and the deeper freedom of the ground of being. The Demiurge is not an enemy — it's a mirror. A warning.

The counterfeit pneuma doesn't come as chaos — it comes as control. Not as darkness, but as sterile light. And the moment we believe it fully, we fall under its spell.

But the story doesn't leave us there. In both ancient mythology and inner life, there is always an answer to the tyrant. In Greek myth, Kronos (Saturn) devours his children out of fear of being overthrown. He is the closed system, the devourer of potential. But Zeus is born in secret and raised beyond the reach of his father — and when he returns, he does not just destroy the old god. He *overcomes* him. Kronos is bound, not erased. A new order is established — not perfect, but more open, more expansive.

The Christ figure performs the same psychic function in the evolution of the Abrahamic God-image. In *Answer to Job*, Jung makes the radical claim: Christ is not merely God's son — he is God's own moral awakening. In the language of the psyche, Christ is what happens when the previously unconscious Yahweh encounters human suffering through His ordeal with Job and is forced to reckon with it. The wrathful, absolute, law-driven God gives way to an image of reconciliation, compassion, and paradox.

Christ doesn't negate Yahweh. He transforms him.

This is why the image of Christ matters — even for the non-believer. Stripped of dogma, the Christ archetype still serves as a living psychic symbol of wholeness: mercy emerging from judgment, eros emerging from law, vulnerability integrated into power. The opposites held together. In alchemical terms, Christ is the *coniunctio oppositorum* — the union of above and below, of divine and human, of suffering and redemption. He is the philosopher's stone hidden inside religious myth — not as a doctrine to be followed but as a pattern to be lived.

We're not talking about historical fact or theological belief. We're talking about symbolic truth — the deep, structuring patterns of the psyche. And whether one is Christian or not, the Christ image stands at a crucial crossroads in the development of human consciousness. He is what comes after the Demiurge. What comes after Saturn. The turning point where the psyche begins to move from law to soul.

And that's exactly why this image is under threat. Because the counterfeit spirit doesn't just arise in the absence of Christ — it often arises in his name. It mimics the form but guts the content. It preaches transcendence but cuts off the roots. It uses the language of love but cannot bear contradiction, sacrifice or suffering. It keeps the symbol but strips it of its depth.

In this sense, the Christ archetype is not optional. It's vital. Because without it — without that deep symbol of inner reconciliation — we fall back under the reign of Saturn. Into rigidity. Into inflation. Into the counterfeit.

In myth, Saturn (or Kronos) devours his children to prevent being overthrown. He is the god of time turned tyrant — not out of malice but fear. A fear of what comes next. This isn't just an old story — it's an image of a psychic force that arises whenever power tries to lock down life itself.

But the myth doesn't end in devouring. Rhea, Saturn's consort, hides her infant Zeus and preserves him in secret. She doesn't confront Saturn; she protects the seed of the future.

This act — subtle, maternal, essential — is the first appearance of a deeper wisdom. The feminine doesn't fight Saturn's domination head-on. It *waits it out*. It carries the future through the crucible.

The pattern repeats in scripture. Mary escapes with the Christ child while Herod — another Saturnian figure — orders the slaughter of infants out of fear. In Revelation, the image becomes symbolic: a woman in labor, crowned with the sun, flees from the dragon who seeks to devour her unborn child. These myths aren't literal. They're maps of the soul. And they point to something crucial at the turning of epochs: that in times of repression, the future always survives through the feminine.

This feminine force isn't passive. It's protective, wise, and world-bearing. In Christian mysticism and Jungian psychology alike, this is Sophia — divine wisdom — who emerges after Christ's incarnation as the living Holy Spirit, the feminine face of the Godhead. Not as institutional religion but as presence: intuitive, hidden, and vital. Sophia is what remains after the revelation. The whisper that carries it forward. She who holds contradiction and complexity — and refuses to collapse mystery into control.

In a world obsessed with speed and spectacle, Sophia's silence is radical. She doesn't perform. She gestates. And without her, transformation becomes impossible — because she is the container in which the new is allowed to *take shape*. The counterforce to the devouring father isn't another war god. It's the pregnant, onyx-skinned mother in exile, keeping the flame alive in the dark. She is Nut, Hathor, Isis, Rhea, Mary. She is the womb of the stars and the fortress of the soul.

As Sophia begins to constellate again in the collective psyche — not as dogma but as a living presence — the symbolic language of the soul becomes essential. And few systems map that psychic landscape with as much depth and antiquity as astrology. Jung once wrote that astrology is "the summation of all the psychological knowledge of antiquity." In other words, it's not magic — it's projection. A symbolic language through which the psyche mirrors itself in the heavens. When we read the stars, we're often just reading ourselves.

Two of the most potent archetypes in this ancient sky-script are Saturn and Jupiter. Saturn represents structure, limit, time, law — the bones of reality. Jupiter, by contrast, is expansion, meaning, potential, trust — the impulse to grow beyond the known. When these two meet in conjunction, as they do in regular twenty-year cycles (and in rarer elemental shifts every two hundred years), something opens psychically. Epochal tensions come to the surface. The outer and inner worlds rearrange themselves.

Historically, Saturn–Jupiter conjunctions have coincided with cultural turning points — moments when old systems die and new paradigms try to be born. But these births are not guaranteed. The conjunction doesn't promise evolution. It only opens the door. And when the Saturnian principle dominates, it can suffocate Jupiter's vision. The future is stalled, not by lack of possibility — but by fear, control, or the refusal to risk growth.

This is the deeper symbolism of our moment: the conjunction has come again, and with it, the question — will structure serve meaning, or swallow it?

Because when Saturn forgets he is not the whole — when the boundary forgets it exists to protect becoming, not prevent it — the result is stagnation disguised as safety, control dressed up as wisdom. It is in these moments that the counterfeit spirit finds its opportunity. It speaks the language of Jupiter — hope, progress, transformation — but its core is hollow, rigid, Saturnian.

And so, the archetypal drama begins to surface not just in symbols and stories but in the lived world. Techno-gnostic fantasies. Political polarization. Hyper-control in the name of health. Spiritual branding. The optimization of the soul. The Saturn–Jupiter conjunction isn't just a historical curiosity or a mythic symbol. It's a living image of where we are — and what we are becoming. Saturn's shadow has not just risen; it has become ambient. Cultural. Invisible by virtue of being everywhere.

The counterfeit spirit we've traced through psyche and myth has found full embodiment in our time. But it no longer needs horns or robes. It wears suits, uniforms, and user interfaces. It sits behind biometric scanners and algorithmic feeds. It governs not from the pulpit but through infrastructure, code, and ideology. It no longer threatens the soul with fire — it renders the soul irrelevant.

We are living through a Saturnian convergence: a moment in which the archetypal force of control, repression, fear of the future, and spiritual ossification is constellating across every domain of life.

Nowhere is this clearer than in the increasingly apocalyptic tone of global politics — particularly in the blood-soaked spirals of the Israel–Palestine conflict. What we are witnessing isn't simply a war of land or policy — it's the unconscious eruption of a shared religious psychosis. Three Abrahamic religions, each with sacred texts and visions that speak of end times and divine conquest, now weaponize their respective identities against one another — while worshiping, in truth, the same god-image: the Demiurge mistaken for the whole.

Zionist extremism, Islamic fundamentalism, and Christian dominionism all orbit around the Saturnian distortion of the divine — the god obsessed with territory, judgment, sacrifice, and law. The god of borders, hierarchies, and thunderbolts.

What unites these factions is not faith — it is fear disguised as certainty. Power disguised as prophecy. And they are pulling the world toward a future no one believes in but everyone is prepared to die for.

In America, this same current manifests through the mythos surrounding Donald Trump — not as a man but as a Saturnian symbol. His "golden age" rhetoric, his fortress-like branding, his appeal to strength, grievance, and glory — it all echoes the oldest father-archetypes in decline. But what makes it even more insidious is his alignment with the technocratic elite — particularly figures like Peter Thiel, Musk, and the wider Silicon Valley priesthood of control.

Thiel's ventures, from Palantir to AI governance ambitions, speak the language of security and progress, but they conceal a deep-seated Saturnian paranoia: a vision of the future that must be locked down, modeled, predicted, and managed from above. In this vision, freedom is too unstable, too human, too alive. Better to entrust the future to surveillance and code than the unpredictable wildness of spirit. The techno-elite, despite their atheism and rationalism, are not post-religious. They are the high priests of a new Saturnian temple — one of cold gods and calculated transcendence.

But this spirit is not confined to governments or boardrooms. It has seeped into culture. It's in the flattening of youth by screens and systems. It's in the dead eyes of the algorithm's favorite creators — those who build their identities on spectacle and repetition, whose souls are optimized out of their own personas. It's in the rituals of productivity, the valorization of branding over becoming, and the casual sacrament of constant surveillance. It's in the influencers, the founders, the talking heads, the CEOs — all becoming archetypes of Saturnian dominance: rigid, controlling, image-obsessed, and terrified of entropy.

Even spirituality hasn't escaped. Psychedelics, once tools for descent and shadow work, are now often dosed in clean, clinical settings to bolster ego, not dissolve it. The dark night of the soul is being edited out in favor of "results." Healing is performance. The divine feminine is turned into pornified aesthetic. Sophia is nowhere to be found.

This is the world the counterfeit spirit prefers: one where truth is managed, the future feared, and freedom reframed as threat. A world of frozen symbols and hollow certainties. And it's not hidden. It is televised, streamed, quantified, monetized, and sold.

The Antichrist, as Jung intuited, is not a single figure. It is a configuration. A mood. A system. It is what happens when we identify with the light and disown the dark — when we confuse control for wisdom, and repression for order. It is not coming — it's already here. Wearing many faces. Speaking many languages. Rewarded by systems that have forgotten the soul.

To name the counterfeit spirit is not to go to war with it. That would only strengthen its grip. The Antichrist, in Jung's view, is not to be exorcised but integrated — seen, understood, and woven back into consciousness.

> We always think that the Christ figure represents the good, the beautiful, and the true. But this is not the psychological truth. Psychologically, Christ is a symbol of the self; and the self is not only the good and beautiful, it is also the worst you can imagine.
> — C.G. Jung

The Antichrist is the shadow of the Christ — the part split off through our one-sided identification with light. Just as the Demiurge in Gnostic thought is a fragment of the Godhead that mistakes itself for the fullness and totality of the Pleroma. This mythic process also mirrors what occurs within the human psyche when the ego mistakes itself for the totality of consciousness, denying its shadow and suppressing its connection to the higher Self. The moment we deny the dark in ourselves, we set it loose in the world, and the image of God reflects it. What we repress does not disappear; it returns disguised as fate, dressed in virtue, weaponized by technological systems and reflected in culture. This is the counterfeit pneuma.

Jungian Paul Levy writes in his brilliant work on the problem of evil, *Wetiko*:

> The evil of wetiko is not just that it feeds on our life force, but that it fools us into identifying with it. It makes us think we are it. Once we recognize it, we take the first step toward disempowering it.

This is the task now: not to flee, not to purify, not to pretend we're above it — but to recognize it. To realize that what is outside is also inside. That the Antichrist spirit lives in the systems we build and the psychic habits we refuse to question.

The true Christ impulse — whether seen theologically, symbolically, or alchemically — doesn't descend to rescue us from the world. It descends into the world. Into matter. Into darkness. It redeems the rejected and makes the broken whole. Jung saw this movement not as a rejection of the old god-image, but its evolution:

> The continuing incarnation of God in the empirical man is the reason why man is indispensable to the completion of the divine image.

That's the deeper work of now: to see the shadow of God in our politics, in our religions, in our technologies — and in ourselves — without collapsing into cynicism or spiritual by-passing.

The seed of the future lies in the places we least want to look. In the systems we've projected our spirit onto. In the fragments of soul scattered beneath the structures of control.

The answer is not resistance but awareness, stewardship, and wholeness. Or we, as humanity, risk incarnating the dark face of God through our unconsciousness. May we never awaken the one who the Gnostics called Saklas, "The Blindness of God."

Conclusion: Light Within the Shadow

I'm not here to tell you what to believe — or even that you need to change your existing beliefs. Throughout this book, I've gone after almost every modern egregore, ideology, and sacred cow: from political dogma to pop spirituality, from institutional religion to tech-bro accelerationism and optimization culture. But I haven't done it from some place above it all. I have my own convictions, my own cultural passions and mythologies that matter deeply to me.

This wasn't written from a pulpit. It was written from the rubble, from the ruins of belief systems that couldn't hold my pain, and from the hollowness of spiritual structures that collapsed under the weight of their own repression.

I don't bring up the phenomenon of the counterfeit spirit to demonize modern people. I bring it up as a plea: look at your own shadow. That's where the danger really lives. Not out there in the "other side," not in the enemy of the week — but in us. If you can begin to walk through life with an eye on your shadow, you are already doing more than most to resist the entropy that this anti-spirit feeds on.

Jung warned us, after the catastrophes of the twentieth century, that when shadow material is not confronted, it erupts into history as destruction. When the unconscious is ignored, it doesn't stay silent — it becomes fate.

I've seen it firsthand. As a little girl sitting in the Backrooms-style Pentecostal churches hidden in strip malls and warehouses — I felt it. The spiritual desperation in the air, the poverty, the hunger for meaning. I watched congregations get whipped into a frenzy, desperate to be touched by something beyond their pain. But that pain was never held. It was bypassed. Co-opted. Transformed into spectacle and profit by men behind pulpits who mistook charisma for divinity.

And it didn't end there. As I moved into the world of journalism and media, I saw it again — the same abject loops. The same unhealed trauma but wearing different clothes. In activist circles, in cultural movements, in New Age spaces. Guilt without integration. Righteousness without humility. Meaning repackaged as marketing.

It hit me hard: this isn't about religion, culture, or identity. It's deeper than that. This is a configuration in the collective unconscious. The counterfeit spirit doesn't belong to one group — it's a universal temptation. And the shadow can possess anyone who refuses to see their own.

But I'm not calling for false synthesis or shallow unity. That's just another mask the counterfeit wears. What I'm talking about is deeper — and slower. When we honestly confront the opposites within ourselves and allow the Self — that capital-S Self that Jung spoke of — to do its mysterious work, something new is born.

That *something* has always been called the Third Thing.

It's the Christ impulse. The alchemical philosopher's stone. The child born of opposing forces. The conjunction. And right now, in this time of fragmentation and exhaustion, we are yearning for it — even if we don't yet have language for it. That child is what the Book of Revelation hints at with the imagery of the pregnant Woman Clothed in the Sun. That new Aeon.

But it can't be forced. It can't be fabricated through willpower or utopian fantasy. It emerges only through inner integration. Through shadow work. Through humility. Through watching, waiting, and bearing the tension between things.

And that's our task: to steward the seed of this future — like Rhea shielding the infant Zeus from the madness of Cronos, like Mary protecting the Christ child from Herod's troops, like the pregnant Woman of the Apocalypse fleeing the dragon in Revelation. To protect the possibility of real reconciliation from the Saturnian spirit — both in the world, and in ourselves.

We midwife a new Aeon — not by burning down the old but by redeeming what still has soul and composting what doesn't. We reunite spirit and matter. We evolve with the God that is still becoming.

The psyche is not a dead mechanism or a random storm of neurons. It is alive — an ecosystem, a temple, a mythopoetic field. And in times like these, when the outer world loses its coherence, the inner world begins to constellate symbols with new urgency — both good and ill.

The way forward is not to discard myth but to engage it consciously. Not to reject the sacred but to allow it to re-emerge — not as superstition or dogma but as inner reality. As Jung wrote:

> We are living in what the Greeks called the kai-ros — the right moment — for a "metamorphosis of the gods," of the fundamental principles and symbols.

What was once sacred, when exiled from consciousness, returns distorted. But if we face the shadow and enter a relationship with the depths of psyche — honestly, humbly — something holy begins to stir again, a new sacred born from integration.

That is the true task of our time: not to return to old forms but to participate in the reanimation of soul — to make room for mystery again.

If this truly is Late-Stage Babylon, then the sacred is not lost — it's underground, dreaming. And it waits to be remembered.

And so, it began — a little girl in a warehouse church, breathing in the sweat of broken prayers, watching spirits rise and fall like stage curtains. I didn't know then what I know now. That those frenzies of light were often masks for unspoken pain. That behind the tongues of angels, there were shadows no one dared name.

Now I am a woman. And I still believe in the Spirit. But not the one that shouts. I believe in the quiet movement beneath things. The cracked surface where something real tries to blossom. The impulse that says: don't perform wholeness — become it.

There is no clean escape from Babylon. But you can leave quietly. One shadow at a time. One illusion at a time. You can walk backward through the smoke until you remember what your soul smelled like before it was burned for someone else's altar.

I have no doctrine to give you. Only this: your shadow is the key. Your pain is the portal for both darkness and light. Protect the child. Walk the long way home. And listen — underneath the collapse, something holy is stirring.

REPEATER BOOKS

is dedicated to the creation of a new reality. The landscape of twenty-first-century arts and letters is faded and inert, riven by fashionable cynicism, egotistical self-reference and a nostalgia for the recent past. Repeater intends to add its voice to those movements that wish to enter history and assert control over its currents, gathering together scattered and isolated voices with those who have already called for an escape from Capitalist Realism. Our desire is to publish in every sphere and genre, combining vigorous dissent and a pragmatic willingness to succeed where messianic abstraction and quiescent co-option have stalled: abstention is not an option: we are alive and we don't agree.